PURSUING MATURITY

the goal of God

DR. BERIN GILFILLAN

Scripture taken marked NKJV are from the New King James Version®. Copyright © 1979, 1980, 1982 by Thomas Nelson. Used by permission. All rights reserved.

Scripture taken marked NLT are from the Holy Bible, New Living Translation, copyright © 1996. Used by persmission of Tyndale House Publishers, Inc., Wheaton, IL 60189. All rights reserved.

Scripture taken marked NIV are from the Holy Bible, New International Version®, NIV® Copyright © 1973, 1978, 1984, 2011 Biblica, Inc.® Used by permission. All rights reserved worldwide.

Scripture taken marked AMP are from the Amplified Bible. Old Testament copyright © 1965, 1987 by the Zondervan Corporation. The Amplified New Testament copyright © 1954, 1958, 1987 by the Lockman Foundation. Used by permission. All rights reserved worldwide.

Scripture taken marked ESV are from The Holy Bible, English Standard Version. ESV® Text Edition: 2016. Copyright © 2001 by Crossway Bibles, a publishing ministry of Good News Publishers. Used by permission. All rights reserved worldwide.

Scripture taken marked MSG are from The Message®. Copyright © 1993, 1994, 1995, 1996, 2000, 2001, 2002 by Eugene H. Peterson. Used by permission. All rights reserved worldwide.

Scripture taken marked KJV are from the King James Version of the Bible, which is under Public Domain.

Scripture taken marked DOUAY-RHEIMS are from the Douay-Rheims 1899 American Edition (DRA) Version of the Bible, which is under Public Domain.

The Science of God: The Convergence of Scientific and Biblical Wisdom by by Gerald L. Schroeder. Copyright © 2009 Free Press; Reprint edition. All rights reserved.

12 Rules for Life: An Antidote to Chaos by Jordan B. Peterson. © 2018 Random House Canada. All rights reserved.

How to Dream When You're Told You're Going to Die by Diego Mesa. © 2014 Diego Mesa. All rights reserved.

All **bolding** and CAPITALIZATION are the emphasis of the author.

Pursuing Maturity: The Goal of God.
Copyright © 2019 Berin Gilfillan
All rights reserved

Publisher: Shepherd's Life
Book Cover Designer: Svyatoslav Romanov
Book Cover Photo by Jeremy Lapak on Unsplash

Editor: Theresa Aguilar
Copyeditor: Corbin Foster

ISBN 978-0-578-46137-3

Shepherd's Life
Redlands, California
https://isom.org/pursuingmaturity/

CONTENTS

Foreword	v
Introduction	vii
Chapter 1: Mandela and Maturity	1
Chapter 2: Maturity: The Goal of God	5
Chapter 3: Hunger and Thirst	9
Chapter 4: Maturity and Defining Moments	17
Chapter 5: The Maturing Process	27
Chapter 6: Maturity and Identity	39
Chapter 7: Mentoring to Maturity	55
Chapter 8: Employment as a Vehicle of Mentoring	63
Chapter 9: Maturity and Discipline	77
Chapter 10: Maturity and Truth	89
Chapter 11: How to Mine Truth: Pilate and the Crucifixion	101
Chapter 12: Maturity and Balance	119
Chapter 13: New Testament Laws	129
Chapter 14: Going on to Full Maturity	157
Chapter 15: A Loyal Heart	167
Conclusion	171
About the Author	173

FOREWORD

Dr. Berin Gilfillan's new book is a masterpiece because he himself is a true man of God inside and out. We have been side-by-side for years, and I saw him develop into an amazingly competent Christian leader. The LORD has given to him and his wife Lisa a ministry called Good Shepherd Ministries, International (GSMI). Through that organization, they have created ISOM, the world's largest video Bible School with a staggering global student body and world faculty. I personally hold them in high esteem and love the whole Gilfillan family. I'm honored and humbled to have had some part in their spiritual development.

Berin observed the multitudes coming to Jesus at my Gospel campaigns and was gripped by God to help those 'seeds of salvation' move to one hundredfold increase. This takes a mighty watering of that seed, and this is why ISOM was created, which I was gladly a part of.

As I have traveled the world, I have met graduates from ISOM, who are now working in their respective God-appointed fields. This is an abundance of fruit.

Pursuing Maturity: The Goal of God comes out of the process Berin has observed all over the world of believers moving from that moment of salvation, so dear to my heart, to that place of mature Christian fruitfulness. I especially recommend his chapter on balance. Even kindness kills when it is out of balance, but goodness is perfection when it is released in a right and proportional way.

What are the ingredients that help make a great man or woman of God?

This is where Berin's book comes in *Pursuing Maturity: The Goal of God*. I highly recommend it.

Evangelist Reinhard Bonnke
Founder of Christ for all Nations (CfaN)

INTRODUCTION

This is not a complicated book. It really has only one major theme, the pursuit of maturity. What is maturity? It is that place of completeness, of fruitfulness and of full measure effectiveness. It's that state of being where an individual has endured the process of time, has weathered the storms and has come to a place of wisdom, experience, and stability in their thinking, their emotions, their walk with God and in their disposition towards life. If that does not define it for you, then hopefully by the end of this easy-to-read book, the full concept, and the importance of it, will become clear.

Why is this topic important? It's because it is central to the purposes of God for any human life. It's the dream of any parent for their child, and it's what every business hopes for in their employees and what every sports coach desires for their athletes. We need to understand how to mold into the lives of people true Christian character, and we need to discover how to more effectively place individuals on a pathway to fulfilling God's will for their lives. So what are the practical elements or ingredients that will help this happen?

I believe we need a generation of believers who are full of conviction but not legalistic, bold but not brash, strong yet gentle. We need multifaceted Christians who are cognizant of their callings, full of vision and purpose, able to articulate their faith and ideas while understanding and respecting the positions and perspectives of others. We need those who can intelligently express their intellect and their emotions, and whose lives reflect the genuine fruit of God's Spirit without hypocrisy or double-mindedness.

This book is about taking you on a journey of thought and of the practical outworking of ideas. It is about helping you to understand that the pursuit of maturity is not an option, but rather a mandate that God has placed over every human life. What is the end game for all of us? It is to facilitate the full development and maturing of ourselves, of those around us, and especially of the next generation of Christian believers.

I have the honor of having developed the world's largest video Bible school called the International School of Ministry (ISOM). We are in over 150 nations, are available in numerous languages, have tens of thousands of schools and hundreds of thousands of students. The program is known for utilizing some of the world's most fruitful Christian leaders as its instructors. People like John Bevere, Jack Hayford, Reinhard Bonnke, Joyce Meyer, Brian Houston, A.R. Bernard, Marilyn Hickey, and many others all contributed to the ISOM's content. We enable and encourage every local church in the world to start within their walls a quality Bible training school, with the objective of developing disciples, leaders, and mature Christian believers. We have been doing this for over 20 years, and I am now more passionate than ever about the goal and the process of helping local churches facilitate the maturing of their congregation members.

The ISOM is a tangible product that flows out of the multiplication principles contained in God's promise to Abraham found in Genesis 22:16–19. I elaborated extensively on those principles in my only other book, *Unlocking the Abraham Promise*. If you have not already read that book, I encourage you to do so as it delves profoundly into the biblical foundations of multiplication growth.

Understanding multiplication principles in the Scriptures is an excellent goal but what is even more valuable is to develop the practical vehicles that will apply those principles into the lives of ordinary people. That is why we have put so much effort into the development of what I call "vehicles of process." These are the tangible curriculum tools that help facilitate the journey to maturity in the lives of individuals.

I used to limit my thinking to just developing people's maturity in their faith (the ISOM), but now believe we need to help people become mature in all facets of life. The passion to see that happen has prompted the development of many additional curriculums including a Women's curriculum, a Marketplace curriculum, a Business Training School program, a Community Development program, a Youth curriculum called YouthBytes and the full curriculum content for a Bachelor's and a Master's degree.

While the practical tools we have developed are helpful, they are only one piece of the puzzle. How do we develop the character of Christ in others? How do we develop greatness of heart and powerful vision in the next generation? The future and success of the Church rests on our ability to make authentic disciples who will reach our world for Jesus Christ.

The current ministry I head up is called Good Shepherd Ministries, International. Even though the burden for this book is connected strongly with all the training programs we have developed, our ministry purpose is much broader than just practical tools. Ultimately we would like to contribute to the larger topic of defining effective elements that advance the Christian journey to maturity. We also would like to be a part of helping to formulate and articulate the philosophical and practical steps behind the mentoring, discipleship and leadership training process.

INTRODUCTION

The purpose of this book is to add another dimension to the equation. Not only should local churches help people understand their faith and grow in it, but it's a pastor, a parent, a leader, a teacher, a friend or a coach who has to add legs to the process and apply truth into the lives of others. Simply put, we want to provide additional wisdom to go alongside instruction to help bring people to maturity.

I had the great privilege of being mentored by one of God's best, Reinhard Bonnke. Being his TV producer and traveling to massive crusades around the world with him for more than three years enabled me to learn an enormous amount from his life. I certainly caught more than I was taught, but that too was a secret of Christ's maturing process. There is hardly a day that goes by when I don't quote or recall a lesson I learned from Reinhard.

Early in this book I cover my own spiritual formation and expand it to encompass a much broader picture. Mentoring is a personal passion of mine and has been so for years. I currently mentor, on a daily basis, not only my two daughters but my staff of over 20 employees and also about a half a dozen young people scattered around the world. Those who live far away I try to email or text on a regular basis, involving myself in their lives, challenges, decisions, and spiritual formation. The growth in God of all these people is perhaps my greatest joy and blessing as a Christian. Mentorship, when driven by the genuine love of Christ, should not be a chore but can become an incredibly rewarding experience. Whether you are being mentored or if you want to learn to mentor others better, you will be challenged and helped by the pages ahead. I will be coming at this whole topic from both a Scriptural and a natural perspective. As I previously mentioned, I have only ever written one other book. I originally described the creation of that first book as being like carrying a baby. I felt if I did not give birth to it, that it would cause great discomfort inside of me. My wife Lisa continually reminds me that I know nothing about the pains of childbearing and it's not an argument I ever want to win. What I do know is that I do not have the ability to write books simply to please a publisher or just to put out something new. What motivates me is the idea of giving birth to a message and sowing something into others that will change their thinking, be highly practical and hopefully bring clarity and direction to people's lives. I hope this book will accomplish just that.

Finally, this book is designed to be very readable, practical and full of amazing stories and anecdotes. I learned to teach by being a children's pastor, overseeing about 1,200 kids who were 12 years old and younger. I have also discovered through the years how to use media and stories to communicate God's Word. I have included a vast number of captivating illustrations and quotes throughout this book, which will hopefully grab your attention and hold it from cover to cover. May you not only enjoy what you read but also may the truths contained in each modern-day parable stick in your mind and in your heart and bring forth lasting fruit in your life. Welcome to *Pursuing Maturity: The Goal of God*.

CHAPTER ONE

Mandela and Maturity

> *"The key to understanding Mandela is those 27 years in prison. The man who walked onto Robben Island in 1964 was emotional, headstrong, easily stung. The man who emerged was balanced and disciplined. I often asked him how the man who emerged from prison differed from the willful young man who had entered it. He hated this question. Finally, in exasperation one day, he said, "I came out mature."*
>
> — Richard Stengel, Managing Editor, *Time Magazine*

Although I have lived in the USA for more than 30 years, I grew up in South Africa, and Nelson Mandela has long been a great hero of mine. I personally feel a sense of gratitude to him for saving the land of my birth from becoming another Rwanda.

My formative years were spent under the heavy hand of apartheid. The ruling National Party was a brutal regime that allowed very little criticism and was a government that put down dissent with an austere and often vicious hand. They built up an impressive military, which I avoided serving in by exercising my US citizenship at the age of 18 and leaving the country. I was not willing to fight for the apartheid system and, in my mind, that meant not making South Africa my future home. Many of my friends ended up in townships shooting at rioting crowds, and some gave their lives fighting on South Africa's borders with other nations.

We all knew the penalties of speaking up against the ruling government. The laws were carefully crafted to create an unfair advantage to the privileged white population and to control and oppress the black majority. We knew of the savage murder of Steve Biko in prison and of the terrible price other dissidents faced who tried to oppose or speak against the laws or governing systems. We also knew that South Africa had strengthened itself to withstand any outside invasion. It had developed nuclear weapons and even a strong air and naval force, in addition to its massive army. Its internal police were brutal, and it seemed from inside and out to be an impenetrable regime.

So when Nelson Mandela, without the firing of a single shot, was able to bring down the apartheid government, it shook the world. From a prison cell, Mandela negotiated the conditions for a new South Africa. He transitioned from a prison to a palace and took over the leadership of a nation. There was nobody else with his stature who could have accomplished what he did, and it was because he had come to a place of "maturity." A few years ago I visited the new Mandela museum, built at the site in KwaZulu Natal where Mandela was captured in 1962. The museum is filled with amazing facts about Mandela's life, but one tribute especially caught my attention. It said the following:

"Missionary Teachers contributed to the building of Mandela's character. They set high standards of morality. An important aspect of Christianity was forgiveness – to harbor grievances would be to lessen one's own character."

Little did those missionaries who taught this principle to the young Nelson Mandela realize that they were contributing to the future saving of a whole nation.

If there was anyone who had a right to be bitter and vengeful about their life, it was Mandela. When he took the reigns of power, he had many encouraging him to get even with his oppressors and with all those who had made life so miserable for the blacks in South Africa. Instead, he chose the undeserved road of forgiveness and reconciliation, and the world has seen few leaders of his stature and significance in the last 100 years. He never held on to power but intentionally served for only five years. He never sought a second term in office even though he fully had the right to do so.

Under Mandela's presidency, welfare spending in South Africa significantly increased. The government introduced parity in grants for communities, including disability grants, child maintenance grants, and old-age pensions, which had previously been set at different levels for South Africa's different racial groups. In 1994, free healthcare was introduced for children under six and pregnant women, a provision extended to all those using primary level public sector health care services in 1996. By the 1999 election, the ANC could boast that due to their policies, three million people were connected to telephone lines, 1.5 million children were brought into the education system, 500 clinics were upgraded or constructed, two million people were connected to the electricity grid, water access was extended to three million people, and 750,000 houses were constructed, housing nearly three million people. These stats are all a tribute to Mandela's influence. The following are four of my favorite Mandela quotes:

> "You will achieve more in this world through acts of mercy than you will through acts of retribution."

> "Know a nation by its jails. Judge a nation not by how it treats its highest citizens, but its lowest ones."

CHAPTER 1: MANDELA AND MATURITY

"Money won't create success, the freedom to make it will."

"To be free is not merely to cast off one's chains, but to live in a way that respects and enhances the freedom of others."

Right after Mandela was released, he visited the USA for the first time. On the way to America, he stopped off in both Libya and Cuba to thank Muammar Gaddafi and Fidel Castro for standing with him during his long years of internment. He then landed in New York and faced a huge town hall meeting organized by ABC News with Ted Koppel as his interviewer. In that incredible television event, Koppel chastised Mandela for having stopped off in Libya and Cuba, two of America's greatest enemies, on his way to his first visit to the USA. Without even flinching, Mandela answered that his actions had no political intention, but were acts of gratitude to two men who had stood by him while he was in prison. He said, "Now that I am free, I will go and say thank you." I remember watching and being deeply impressed with Mandela's principled stand despite its political ramifications in the USA.

Mature people like Mandela do great things for society. They also achieve a high degree of personal fulfillment. There are many contributing factors along life's journey that contribute to the maturing process. Time, defining moments, training, literature, education, key relationships, personal discipline, exposure to other great people, experience, and many other factors are key to helping people along the journey. We will look at many of these fascinating components in the pages ahead. Many of these are components to which you would not expect someone like Mandela to have had access, yet he used every opportunity and ended up succeeding.

I often correlate the life of Mandela with the biblical story of Joseph. He too came out of prison and went to a place of powerful influence in a palace. Those difficult experiences in a dungeon did not end up defining either Joseph nor Mandela. Both leaders instead kept the guiding principles of their lives strong, their integrity intact and they let their experiences and hardships mold their character and mature them. They both prove the point that you can either let the experiences and hardships of life define and destroy you, or you can let them mold and make you. It is fascinating to me that in the opening quote of this chapter by Richard Stengel of *Time Magazine*, that he would hone in on "maturity" as the one facet of Mandela's character that would help people to understand his growth to greatness. Stengel spent more than a year with Mandela working on his autobiography *Long Walk to Freedom: The Autobiography of Nelson Mandela* and subsequently did an outstanding second book *Mandela's Way: Fifteen Lessons on Life, Love and Courage* as well as serving as co-producer of the documentary film *Mandela* which ended up being nominated for an Academy Award®.

Because the target audience of this book is primarily Christians, I will draw a good bit of inspiration in the pages ahead from Bible characters such as Joseph and from key Scriptural passages. One of the greatest criticisms I hear about people of faith is that they are sometimes extreme and unbalanced. It is also true that many are unable to articulate their faith in a way that makes sense to the rest of society. Hopefully, this book will inspire Christians to pursue a place of balance, discipline, and wisdom. A place, like Mandela, of "maturity." Let's close this chapter by once again looking at our opening quote:

> *"The key to understanding Mandela is those 27 years in prison. The man who walked onto Robben Island in 1964 was emotional, headstrong, easily stung. The man who emerged was balanced and disciplined. I often asked him how the man who emerged from prison differed from the willful young man who had entered it. He hated this question. Finally, in exasperation one day, he said, "I came out mature."*
>
> — Richard Stengel, Managing Editor, *Time Magazine*

CHAPTER TWO

Maturity: The Goal of God

*My little children, for whom I labor in birth again
until Christ is formed in you.*

— Apostle Paul (Galatians 4:19 NKJV)

Maturity is a God idea. Although Jesus does emphasize that a person needs to have childlike faith, He does not promote childish faith. It is not His intent to have a kingdom full of Peter Pans. His goal for each of us is that we grow up to be like Him. I heard a humorous tale of a minister who was having terrible troubles getting along with his wife. Finally, in exasperation, he prayed "LORD, can't you change her and make her a bit more compatible and like me." He got a quick response from up above, "If I make her more compatible and like you, I'm going to have an even more difficult time making her more compatible and like me." The point is God wants all of us to become more like Jesus.

The Apostle Paul writes in Ephesians 4:13 NLT that *"we will **be mature** in the LORD, measuring up to the full and complete standard of Christ."* Paul goes on to describe this process as involving the active participation of all of the five-fold ministry:

> Now these are the gifts Christ gave to the church: the apostles, the prophets, the evangelists, and the pastors and teachers. Their responsibility is to equip God's people to do his work and build up the church, the body of Christ. This will continue until we all come to such unity in our faith and knowledge of God's Son that we will be **mature in the LORD**, measuring up to the full and complete standard of Christ. Then **we will no longer be immature like children** (Ephesians 4:11–13 NLT).

We will discuss in a later chapter the powerful impact of other people and the five-fold ministry gifts in our growth to maturity, but Paul in this section goes on to give us the ultimate objective of this process two verses later: *"But, speaking the truth in love, **may grow up in all things** into Him who is the head – Christ"* (Ephesians 4:15 NKJV).

God's objective for every Christian is that we would *"grow up in all things"* and become like Christ. In the New Testament, there is this wonderful description of young Jesus' growth process before the nation of Israel: *"And Jesus increased in wisdom and stature, and in favor with God and men"* (Luke 2:52 NKJV).

5

In the famous 1 Corinthians 13 love chapter, Paul wrote, *"When I was a child, I spoke as a child, I understood as a child, I thought as a child; but when I became a man, I put away childish things"* (1 Corinthians 13:11 NKJV). Although Paul still did not understand everything and admitted in the same chapter that he *"saw in a mirror dimly,"* he did acknowledge that he was moving to the day when he would see Jesus *"face to face"* and *"know"* just as he also was known.

The writer of the book of Hebrews talks about a person's ability to digest profound teaching. He says, *"so let's stop going over the basic teachings about Christ again and again. Let us go on instead and **become mature** in our understanding"* (Hebrews 6:1 NLT).

In any sphere of study, there is a progression towards a mature understanding. One of my good friends is a radiologist. He spent 13 years of academic study pursuing the field of medicine. He now has a mature understanding of a tiny area of the brain that few others could diagnose. Mature scientists attend conferences where information is shared that the majority of the public wouldn't even begin to comprehend. However, it is in the hands of these scientists that breakthroughs in technology happen. From their mature minds come the latest and greatest mobile devices, painkillers, and cures for major diseases. The greatest fruitfulness in people's lives lies at the point of maturity.

In the New Testament, the Apostle Paul longed to relate to Christian believers in a mature way. He longed to go deeper with them and to unpack spiritual mysteries. He wanted to share with them the ancient types and shadows from the Old Testament, things like the tabernacle, the covenants and the meanings of the feasts of Israel. He writes *"Yet when I am among **mature** believers, I do speak with words of wisdom, but not the kind of wisdom that belongs to this world or to the rulers of this world, who are soon forgotten"* (1 Corinthians 2:6 NLT).

Later in the same letter of 1Corinthians, he writes *"Dear brothers and sisters, don't be childish in your understanding of these things. Be innocent as babies when it comes to evil, but **be mature** in understanding matters of this kind"* (1 Corinthians 14:20 NLT).

The point is that maturity is a very biblical concept. Even the parable of the sower in the Gospels has this concept built into it. The objective of that story is what happens after the seed matures. Some seeds get choked to death, and others multiply by 10,000% (a hundredfold). For those not good at the math, if one seed produced a second seed, that would be a 100% return or a doubling of the original seed. If one seed produced ten seeds that would be 1,000% return. So if one seed produced 100 seeds, that would be a 10,000% return. The secret revealed in this parable is that the quality of soil, or the condition of the heart, on which the word of God lands determines its fruitfulness.

Jesus spent 30 years preparing for his earthly ministry, and a lot of that was spent studying the Scriptures and developing His human understanding of the world. Only when His preparation was mature did He then spend three years doing ministry. Most people going into ministry work spend three years preparing for 30 years of ministry work. It is clear who got the pattern right.

For Jesus, the maturity of His calling was the cross. Everything in His life led up to that last 24 hours from the Last Supper through the crucifixion. Had He not been mature enough in His preparation and had He not brought his calling to completion, we would NOT HAVE the salvation we enjoy today. The maturing of our lives and calling can affect millions of people.

It is interesting that the word in the Greek for *mature* is often translated in the New and Old King James versions as the word *perfect*.

Here are a few examples of how different versions of the Bible translate this word *perfect*:

> Therefore, leaving the discussion of the elementary *principles* of Christ, let us go on to **perfection**, not laying again the foundation of repentance from dead works and of faith toward God. (Hebrews 6:1 NKJV)

> So let us stop going over the basic teachings about Christ again and again. Let us go on instead and **become mature** in our understanding. Surely we don't need to start again with the fundamental importance of repenting from evil deeds and placing our faith in God. (Hebrews 6:1 NLT)

> For we are glad, when we are weak, and ye are strong: and this also we wish, even your **perfection**. (2 Corinthians 13:9 KJV)

> We are glad to seem weak if it helps show that you are actually strong. We pray that you will become **mature**. (2 Corinthians 13:9 NLT)

PURSUING MATURITY

> To whom God would make known what is the riches of the glory of this mystery among the Gentiles; which is Christ in you, the hope of glory: Whom we preach, warning every man, and teaching every man in all wisdom; that we may present **every man perfect** in Christ Jesus. (Colossians 1:27-28 KJV)

> To them God has chosen to make known among the Gentiles the glorious riches of this mystery, which is Christ in you, the hope of glory. He is the one we proclaim, admonishing and teaching everyone with all wisdom, so that we may present everyone **fully mature** in Christ. (Colossians 1:27-28 NIV)

From these Scriptures, it is very clear that the Apostle Paul had the MATURITY or PERFECTING of God's people as the absolute central goal of his work. He knew he would have to present God's people someday before the throne of God, and the measure would be their maturity. The pursuit of maturity for EVERY believer is the GOAL OF GOD.

In Matthew 5:48 NKJV Jesus says, "*Therefore you shall be **perfect**, just as your Father in heaven is **perfect**.*"

I like the way The Message translation puts this verse of Jesus. I will make this the concluding verse of this chapter because I don't know how it could be said any better:

*"In a word, what I'm saying is, **Grow up**. You're kingdom subjects. Now live like it. Live out your God-created identity. Live generously and graciously toward others, the way God lives toward you"* (Matthew 5:48 MSG).

It is obvious that Jesus wants us to produce enormous fruit for Him and come to a place of great maturity, but where do we start? Let's begin by looking at the disposition of heart that a person needs to have in order to receive from God. We will then look at those defining moments in our lives that change and alter our destiny, those places and times and experiences where the seeds of greatness and calling are planted into our hearts. Let's start with our appetite for the things of God.

CHAPTER THREE

Hunger and Thirst

"A *boss makes people to eat, a leader makes them hungry.*"

— Peter Tarkkonen

I remember a children's church teacher once illustrating the principle of spiritual hunger. Right before church started, he ordered a piping hot pizza loaded with lots of delicious toppings. When it was delivered into the classroom, he made sure the aroma filled the room. He then proceeded to take the first slice out of the box and eat the entire piece right in front of the children, pausing between each bite to make another silent emphasis in his message. The kids were barely listening at this stage, their eyes were glued on the pizza, their stomachs were rumbling, and their mouths were salivating. Much to their dismay, the teacher ate the whole pizza without giving them any. The teacher then related to them how their hunger for God needed to be at least as great as their hunger for that pizza. It certainly was a moment and a lesson that none of them will soon forget.

Opportunity is not as important as appetite. The Scriptures say that those who hunger and thirst after righteousness will have that desire fulfilled. Specifically, Jesus says: *Blessed are* those who hunger and thirst for righteousness, *for they shall be filled* (Matthew 5:6 NKJV). There is something about spiritual hunger that touches the heart of God, but He is also the source of all good appetites and of all good forms of hunger.

Chris Baker – Mott Children's Hospital
When I was at the University of Michigan, I had a profound experience that has impacted my life ever since. I wanted to do something to practically demonstrate my faith on the campus, so I volunteered at the University Mott Children's Hospital. I worked with a guy called Nick who was in charge of the Activities Department. I would go to play games with the sick kids and often just visit those in their wards who were too sick to come to the Activity Room.

One day, as I was going to different wards visiting kids, I came into a room and saw a nine-year-old boy lying there by the name of Chris Baker. Since he was born, Chris had probably spent more time in hospitals than he had at home because he had a rare blood disease called aplastic anemia. After trying many drugs, the doctors finally did a bone marrow transplant, and Chris was recovering from that very dangerous procedure. The moment I saw Chris, I had a deep love and desire come in my heart to get to know him and to become a friend and a mentor to his life. The desire was so strong that it surprised me. That evening I said to a friend going into our Campus Christian Fellowship Meeting, "Could anything I want this much be from God. Is this just me or is this God?"

After the Fellowship meeting, three of us went back to a home I was house sitting to fellowship and pray. One of those who went with me was my future wife Lisa, but at that point, we were just great Christian friends. Now the Lord uses Lisa powerfully in the prophetic and, as we prayed, she spoke a wonderful prophetic word over the third person who had joined us. I had not said a word to Lisa about my hospital experience earlier in the day, but after hearing the other prophetic word, I looked at her and asked tentatively, "Does the Lord have a word for me?"

I will never forget Lisa's answer. She said, "There is something that you have been saying 'Could anything I want this much be from God?'" She literally quoted the words I had spoken three hours earlier to another person, and she knew NOTHING about what I had said. Then she said, "I don't know what it is, but I can see the Lord on His throne smiling and saying 'This is what it means when I say in My Word: *Delight yourself also in the Lord, And He shall give you the desires of your heart*" (Psalms 37:4 NKJV). I will not just give you what you want, but **I will give you the right things to want**.'"

God was literally saying to me that He would put the RIGHT desires inside of me if I will delight myself in Him. He will put the hunger for Him inside of us if we ask for it. That was the green light I needed to start ministering to Chris Baker, and God began to restore Chris's health from that point forward. Over the next three years, I truly learned how to sow into the lives of young people through the friendship and mentorship relationship I had with Chris. It was driven by a supernatural love and caring that God placed in my heart when I met him. He ended up being a groomsman in our wedding when Lisa and I tied the knot about five years later. Chris lived until he was 26 years old before he succumbed to pneumonia and the Lord took him home.

Human beings are driven with passions and desires from within. Anyone running a coed boarding school will be continually amazed at the ingenious ways teens will devise in order to connect because they are internally attracted to each other. Just the desire to win a gold medal can drive Olympic athletes through punishing training. Internally they are hungry for the fame and glory that winning will bring them. The greater their appetite for success, the more they will be driven to practice grueling routines.

At one time John D. Rockefeller was the richest man in the world, yet he would continue to work extremely hard. Someone once asked him, "Why do you keep working yourself so hard, how much money will be enough for you?" His answer was telling, "Just a little more [. . .]" Such is the deceptive drive of greed. There are some things the Bible tells us are insatiable, like the barren womb. The only thing that will satisfy that desire is the birth of a child.

Insatiable hunger can drive people to do wonderful things and terrible things. The Old Testament tells us that in the midst of certain lengthy sieges, where all food had been depleted, some parents did the unthinkable by eating their own children. Other parents are driven to crime to take care of their families. The point is that unless a person is driven by a desire from within, they will often not last long in any voluntary endeavor. When they are driven by a desire for success, hunger, security, acceptance, love, sex, thirst or to simply break a record or cross a new frontier, they will often do things that will astound others.

So why would it be any different when it comes to spiritual hunger? As I mentioned in the introduction to this book, many years ago I had the privilege of being the television producer for the famous German evangelist Reinhard Bonnke. It was in the days just before his ministry began driving upwards of a million people in a single crusade meeting. When I was with Reinhard, crowds ranged between 20,000 and about 200,000, which was still a lot. During those three years, I remember two distinct incidents relating to spiritual hunger that massively impacted my life. One took place at my first crusade experience after joining his team and the other at my last.

Sekondi-Takoradi: First Gospel Crusade with Reinhard Bonnke
The first incident took place in western Ghana, in the small town of Sekondi-Takoradi. I was greatly intrigued by Reinhard's simple preaching of the Gospel and by the huge reaction of the crowds to his story-filled messages. I also specifically remember capturing for the first time a blind person being healed. You would have thought I was overjoyed but, as a television producer, I wasn't. You see Reinhard prayed for about fifty blind people on the third night of the crusade and only about five received their sight. This disturbed me greatly because I had my camera focused on some of those who were not healed.

Seeing their disappointed faces troubled my heart and the following afternoon I was knocking at Reinhard's door. I had to ask him, "What about those who did NOT get healed?" His answer has helped me until today. He said in his strong and distinctive accent, "Berin, you can either look at what God is doing or at what He isn't doing. It is better that we prayed in faith for all the blind people, and five of them can now see who couldn't see before than if we didn't pray for any of them and nobody got their sight back."

Later back in Germany I heard Reinhard say that he was glad that not everyone was healed at his meetings. "We would never have rest day or night if everyone got healed," he said, and he was right. As it was, people who heard of the miracles and healings through his meetings often came to his headquarters in Germany for prayer.

Well, back to the hunger incident in Sekondi-Takoradi. As we concluded six glorious nights of meetings, the crusade team began packing up the stage, the sound system, and the lights. It was at that point that a small group of people arrived at the crusade ground. When we interviewed them, we discovered that they had been walking for a full week to get to the crusade meetings and had arrived right after the final meeting was over.

It stunned me. In many countries, people will barely walk a mile to a grocery store or will struggle to wake up early to pray or read their Bible. The thought of walking a WEEK to hear the word of God is unthinkable to most in the West. It was then that I understood why God was doing so many great things in Africa. It was in response to this kind of deep spiritual hunger. We laid hands and prayed for these precious African people but felt devastated that they had missed the crusade meetings.

First Gospel Crusade in 70 Years in the Former Soviet Union
My final crusade with Reinhard's ministry was about 3½ years later. It was mid-1989 and was very likely the first Gospel crusade meeting held in 70 years in the former Soviet Union. The opportunity came about because the Baltic States were, at that time, beginning to flex their muscles against Moscow. Somehow, the Latvian state officials allowed the Christians to book the famous outdoor Mesa Amphitheater in the city of Riga. Reinhard and his team had just gotten back into Germany from a crusade in Uganda, and six of our passports were rushed to the Russian Embassy in Bonn for the necessary visas.

When we received back the passports in Frankfurt, we discovered that all of us had been granted visas except for Reinhard. This was Moscow's way of trying to block this event. An emergency meeting was held at Reinhard's Frankfurt headquarters, and it was decided that the team would go anyway and Reinhard officially handed the crusade over to his right-hand man, Reverend Peter Van den Berg.

As we boarded the Lufthansa flight for Moscow, Peter began to feel sick. By the time we landed in Moscow, he was showing signs of full-blown malaria. First, Reinhard was out because of no visa, and now Peter had a serious medical condition. I was sorely hoping that I was not going to be tapped to do the preaching. I was mature then as a television producer but certainly not as a crusade preacher. As it was, I was taking in amateur TV recording equipment so as to not draw the KGB's attention to my video documentation of that historic event.

The good news is that after about 72 hours, God raised Peter up from his sick bed and he did an amazing job of preaching to over 10,000 Russian-speaking people who attended the crusade. In the middle of the event, God gave an incredible prophecy through Peter. Remember it was the Soviet Union at that time and it had been CLOSED to the Gospel for 70 years. This is what God said to the Russian speaking nations:

> "I have heard your cry, says the LORD. I have listened to your call for a long time, says the LORD. But the time for crying is passed, the time for waiting is over, says the LORD. But the time of the outpouring of my Spirit has begun, and I shall move upon you, and I shall move upon your children, and you shall know the move of my Spirit upon your leaders, and in your churches, and in your homes, and in your factories, and in your schools. I shall move by my Spirit, says the LORD. For this is the day that the prophets have talked of when I shall pour of my Spirit upon all flesh. Know that your time of crying is over, that your time of waiting is passed, and the time of rejoicing has begun, says the LORD."

A few months later the Berlin wall was torn down, and the breakup of the former Soviet Union officially began. Although that 1989 prophecy was incredible, what sealed the significance of that event for me was the reaction of the believers and the leaders on the platform in Riga. The Christians literally stood looking over the crowd of more than 10,000 pressing in to hear the Word of God and said, "How many of our brothers and sisters in Siberia wept tears to see this day when the Word of God would once again be proclaimed openly." Those who have read Alexander Solzhenitsyn's book *The Gulag Archipelago*, or who in any way had contact with the former Soviet Union's tactics and methods, will deeply understand the sentiment of these believers.

That Riga event, combined with the changing political climate during that season, opened a floodgate of church planting and evangelism all across the Russian-speaking world. The Soviet Union literally had experienced a seventy-year famine where the Word of God was extremely rare. That famine of God's Word fueled ministries like Brother Andrew's Open Doors and many others who brought Bibles into the nation. What a privilege to witness the very beginnings of that breaking of the Soviet dam and the start of that amazing new move of God. I produced a report for the *700 Club®*, which the Christian Broadcasting Network® immediately broadcast worldwide. From my first crusade in Second Takoradi to my last in Riga, Latvia in the former Soviet Union, the message was the same. The heartfelt hunger of God's people for truth and an understanding of His Word opened a floodgate in the heavens to meet that hunger.

Outward Bound
When it comes to the pursuit of maturity, hunger and thirst are key parts. When I was a boy growing up in South Africa, I remember seeing a movie produced by a group called Outward Bound. My brother Graeme was going on one of their trails, and the movie was shown to prepare those who were about to encounter that grueling experience.

The movie started at daybreak on a hot African day. Each camper was forced by the trail leader to empty their water bottles, and a long trek in the blazing sun was begun. By early afternoon, the parched group was at the point of collapsing, and people's tongues were sticking to the roofs of their mouths. A few hours later after a further grueling climb up a high mountain in the unrelenting afternoon heat, the group of incredibly thirsty teenagers came to a vantage point that gave them the first look of a river way down in the valley below. So desperate were these young people for water that they literally began running down that mountainside towards the water. Watching those teenagers run towards that river and dive in to drink its fresh waters is an image I will never forget. The movie closed with one of the Outward Bound instructors explaining to the group how valuable water is in the wild.

Many years ago, an indigenous bushman from the Kalahari Desert area of South Africa was taken from an extreme wilderness area, where they typically live and given a tour around the modern city of Cape Town. The Bushmen normally eke out their existence in harsh desert conditions. To get water, they actually take the dew on the plant leaves in the early morning and collect it drop by drop into ostrich eggs so they can survive another day.

Showing this bushman around a modern city was an absolute culture shock for this poor guy. They showed him everything from cars to computers to elevators and modern buildings. When asked at the end of the tour what the most amazing thing he had seen was, he immediately pointed to a water faucet. What a miracle it was for him to be able to turn a simple faucet and get life-giving water! His perspective was driven by his value system—and water was near the top of his list of treasures.

Let's close this chapter with a look at Proverbs 2, where Solomon instructs his son on how to obtain wisdom and to gain understanding. Focus on the words I have **bolded**:

> My son, if you receive my words,
> And **treasure** my commands within you,
> So that you **incline** your ear to wisdom,
> And **apply** your heart to understanding;
> Yes, if you cry out for discernment,
> And lift up your voice for understanding,
> If you **seek** her as silver,
> And **search** for her as for hidden treasures;
> Then you will understand the fear of the Lord,
> And find the knowledge of God (Proverbs 2:1–5 NKJV).

What I believe God is saying here through Solomon is that all of us need to cultivate a deep hunger for the things of God. There is a drive in these highlighted words. They are not passive but rather active requirements that need to come from hungry and inquiring hearts. This is why this book is called *PURSUING Maturity*. There has to be an active pursuit of God and His MATURE ways. These words of Solomon echo some of the phrases that Jesus reiterated in the New Testament when He said the following choice phrases in His famous Sermon on the Mount in Matthew 7:

> [. . .] Seek, and you will find [. . .] (Matthew 7:7 NKJV).

And back to our opening proof Scripture for this chapter. *He who hungers and thirsts for righteousness shall be filled* (Matthew 5:6 NKJV).

And I want to add two more Scriptures from the Old Testament before closing this chapter:

> But from there **you will seek** the Lord your God, **and you will find** *Him* if **you seek** Him with **all your** heart **and** with **all your soul** (Deuteronomy 4:29 NKJV).

> **And you will seek** Me **and find** *Me,* when **you** search for Me with **all your heart** (Jeremiah 29:13 NKJV).

That's also why Peter Tarkkonen says in the opening quote to this chapter: "A boss makes people to eat, a leader makes them hungry."

CHAPTER FOUR

Maturity and Defining Moments

I [Paul] planted, *Apollos watered, but GOD gave the increase.*

— 1 Corinthians 3:6 ESV

The growth of any great plant starts with a singular event, the planting of a seed. In a similar way, maturity in our lives often starts with strategic and significant decisions or experiences that have so much lasting impact that they end up defining our lives.

For me, my wedding vows were a defining moment, but choosing who to make those vows with was no easy decision. I remember wrestling with the weight of this decision while I was in my final year at Regent University, studying for a Master's degree in television and film. My huge question was "How can you be sure it's the right girl?" The statistics were not good. I understood that over 50% of all marriages end in divorce, even in the church world. I was terrified of making the wrong choice and then living a life of regret.

So, for advice, I went to a respected professor of mine at Regent, Dr. Bob Schihl. He was formerly a celibate Catholic priest but, after studying the Scriptures, he concluded that the celibacy mandate of the Catholic Church for priests, was unscriptural. He ended up choosing to get married and had a happy wife and family. I knew he had grappled with this subject both theologically and practically.

Dr. Bob was also approachable and always impressed me with his wisdom so I put to him the question I was wrestling with, "How can you be sure it's the right girl when you go into a wedding ceremony?" At the time I was not satisfied with his answer but later discovered it to be true. He said, "After you say your vows and turn to walk down the aisle, then you will know if it is the right girl." My initial reaction was "that's too late."

When, in 1985, I married my wonderful wife Lisa, I finally understood the wisdom of Dr. Bob's advice. You see your future with a spouse is built upon that defining moment. It is a covenant that you are entering into, and you cannot tell ahead of time what it will be like when you make it. Before I said my vows, I was terrified and stiff as a board. After I made them, I knew I had made the right decision, and we have had a wonderfully happy marriage spanning over three decades at the time of writing this book. The point is that the vow becomes the foundation of a future together.

You cannot make the vow tentatively or on a trial basis. It has to be a permanent commitment, a defining moment upon which you build a new future. Anything less will seed a marriage with uncertainty. This is not to condemn those who have been through the tragedy of divorce but very often, one party or the other, enters the marriage covenant with a flawed understanding of this critical defining moment concept.

My Greatest Defining Moment
Defining moments establish the foundation of your future. Probably the greatest defining moment for any Christian is the decision to fully surrender their life to Christ. This life-altering decision happened to me in 1974 in a stone chapel at Hilton College in KwaZulu-Natal, South Africa. I was a 12-year-old boy attending an all-boys boarding school, and it was my first year of high school. Being at an Anglican school, chapel was a regular part of our daily regimen. It was largely a traditional experience with hymns, readings and a short sermon that most boys had become experts at tuning out. I was probably the only boy that night who experienced a radical defining moment with God, and I certainly didn't understand then that my life would never be the same again.

To this day I don't even know who the preacher was that Sunday night. Most chapel services took place on weekday or Sunday mornings (six times a week). Only once or twice a month did we have what they called an Evensong on a Sunday night. The added entertainment for the boys in an evening service was to watch the bats fly back and forth among the wooden rafters in the high vaulted ceilings of the stone chapel. It was quite the task for a preacher to hold the attention of close to 400 mostly jaded teens, largely inoculated against religion, especially with a bat air show above competing for their attention.

But for some reason, this unknown preacher had my attention that night. Somehow I understood in that service that Christ had died personally for my sins and that He was offering me eternal life if I would receive him into my heart as Lord and Savior. Because it's seldom done in an Anglican church, there was no altar call but simply a closing prayer where those who wanted to respond could voluntarily silently participate. After quietly praying that prayer under my breath with the minister, the service was over, and we were dismissed into the night.

One of the few genuine Christians I knew in the school was a boy named Ashley Williams. A few years later he died of leukemia, but that night he was there for me. I literally said to him "Ashley, I'm not sure what just happened, but I feel such a peace."

He turned to me and said, "You just got born again." "What's that?" I responded. From that day to this, more than 40 years later, I've had a genuine relationship with Christ. It was a defining moment that altered the very course of my life. I still don't know who the preacher was that night. I think he probably considered the evening a bit of a disaster because in the following five years I don't remember ever seeing him again. He was likely discouraged and probably told his wife there was no response and that nobody thanked him or even shook his hand after the service. I'm sure it seemed to him that the boys were more interested in the bats in the ceiling than in his message and I certainly don't think he suspected that somebody had actually gotten "saved."

One day in Heaven I want to find that preacher and shake his hand and thank him for his obedience that 1974 night. Little did he know that through his words, an eternal seed landed on the heart of a 12-year-old boy. I want him to know that he has a share in all the fruit of our ministry that currently is in more than 150 nations and yearly touches the lives of hundreds of thousands of people. Such is the power of a defining moment in a single person's life, and I'm just a small example.

Medical Missionary Dr. Daniel Fountain
A few years ago we recorded a famous medical missionary by the name of Dr. Daniel Fountain. He was a friend of the former US Surgeon General, Dr. C. Everett Coop, and was in his 80's when he recorded with us. So vast was his knowledge that we were able to get more than 20 teaching sessions from him on how to help poor communities in developing countries to get clean water, to develop self-sustaining agriculture and even how to deliver a child into the world when there is no doctor around. Those recordings became a part of our Community Development curriculum called CDBoks. Boks stands for "Building Others through Knowledge and Service."

I was fascinated by Dr. Daniel Fountain's life story and especially about his 35 years as a missionary doctor in the country of the Democratic Republic of the Congo. Our family had been missionaries for about two years in a dangerous region of Nigeria, and I knew that committing one's life to working in those parts of the world is not a decision a person makes lightly. When Dr. Fountain was recording with us, I asked him how he knew he was called to that very difficult part of the world. His story powerfully illustrates the impact of a defining moment.

When Daniel Fountain was only four years old, he was diagnosed with tuberculosis and literally had to spend a year confined to his bed at home. His father was a pastor and this year of isolation was very difficult for the young Daniel. During the course of that year, a number of visiting ministers came to his father's church to preach. Very often his father would have the visiting ministers stay at their home, not only to be hospitable but also to try and keep costs down.

One minister who stayed at their home during that isolating year was a missionary to the Congo. Young Daniel, because of his condition, was unable to attend the service where the missionary shared all of his front-line stories and presented his slide presentation on the Congo to the congregation. However, when he came back to their home to spend the night, this missionary's heart went out to the young, sickly Daniel. To encourage the young boy, he brought his little slide projector into Daniel's room, and there he projected his presentation about the Congo onto a blank wall with the little boy next to him. There, at the age of four, young Daniel Fountain had a defining moment and made a life-long decision to become a missionary to the Congo. He ended up becoming a medical missionary to the Congo for 35 years. He built hospitals and established clinics, and now the knowledge he learned is going around the world through our CDBoks program.

Scripture is full of these defining moments. Take, for example, the anguished prayer of Hannah for a son in 1 Samuel after decades of barrenness. She literally prayed:

> "O LORD of hosts, if You will indeed look on the affliction of Your maidservant and remember me, and not forget your maidservant, but will give your maidservant a male child, then I will give him to the LORD all the days of his life" (1 Samuel 1:11 NKJV).

God granted her request, and young Samuel was born. His mother weaned the young child and then gave him into the service of God by dropping him off at the place where Israel's high priest ministered. Samuel grew up to be one of Israel's greatest prophets, but it was a defining moment in his mother's life that set him on that path. Very often defining moments come out of desperate prayers as in the case of Hannah. She vowed a radical commitment of her child to God if He would answer her desperate prayer.

Dr. Andrew Sherwood
Before I was born, my dad's brother, Graeme Gilfillan, was killed at the age of 19 in a tragic motorcycle accident. It happened on the day he was accepted to medical school at Cambridge University in England. He was only going 25 miles an hour when a friend across the road waved to him. Momentarily distracted, he waved back just as a bus in front of him braked sharply. He tried to veer to the side but hit the bus, was thrown 25 feet onto a sidewalk, breaking his neck. Some hours later, with my father and other family members gathered around his hospital bed, he passed away.

So devastating was this loss to the family that my grandfather, Noel Gilfillan, had a rugby stadium built at Hilton College in memory of my uncle Graeme. He also made the decision to pay the high school and university fees for three aspiring medical school students in memory of his son.

One of those three students, who our family got to know best, was Dr. Andrew Sherwood. He ended up practicing obstetrics in Cape Town. When I was considering becoming a medical doctor, I spent two nights at Cape Town's Groote Schuur hospital with Andrew watching him perform natural childbirths and cesarean sections on a number of patients. This was the same hospital where Dr. Christian Barnard performed the first heart transplant. From my observation, it was obvious that Dr. Sherwood was an outstanding doctor who cared deeply for his patients. However, to cope with the high stress of the job, Andrew developed a nasty habit of cigarette chain smoking.

One of Dr. Andrew's patients who became pregnant was a 44-year-old woman. Although she and her husband had tried for years to conceive, they had NEVER had a child, and so this pregnancy at the age of 44 was incredibly precious. Andrew had overseen her full pregnancy, and she had finally reached full term and come in for the delivery. She was in the process of dilating, and they hooked the child up to a heart monitor. Dr. Andrew had been working long hours and needed to get a shower and a few hours of rest before delivering the child. He went home near midnight but was woken in the wee hours of the morning with a frantic phone call from the hospital that the heartbeat from the child had been lost and those monitoring mother and child were fearing the worst.

Although not a deeply religious person, as Dr. Andrew raced at high speed to the hospital, he prayed a simple prayer "God, if you will save the life of this child, I will never smoke another cigarette again in my life." Only God knows the details of all that happened and how it happened but that heartbeat revived, and a few hours later a healthy child was born. To this day Dr. Andrew Sherwood has never smoked another cigarette. It was a defining moment in his life where he prayed a desperate prayer to God and he, like Hannah, kept the commitment in prayer that he had made.

Dr. Ben Carson Impacted by his Mother Sonya
In recent years people in the USA have been inspired by the life story of Dr. Ben Carson. Many know his fame as a neurosurgeon, a presidential candidate, and a politician. Few really know how a defining moment in his mother's life set him on that path. When Ben was 11 and his brother Curtis was 13, they brought home horrible report cards from school showing them both failing and at the bottom of their classes. Their mother, Sonya, wept and made a decision to take three days to ask God for help and guidance in getting her children on the right path. God showed her to do three

things: 1) not allow the boys to go out to play until they had done their homework; 2) have the boys only watch two hours of television a week and have her choose the content of what they watched; and 3) have the boys visit the local library once a week, choose two books, read them and write a weekly book report on them. She didn't tell them she did not know how to read herself because of her lack of education, but she filled their book reports with red marks anyway. This defining moment, which she refused to budge from, changed the destiny of her children's lives.

In one year the two Carson boys went from the bottom of their classes to the top of their classes. Ben got a full scholarship to Yale University and then got into medical school at the University of Michigan, which is where my wife and I both attended and met. Ben went on to become the head of pediatric neurosurgery at John's Hopkins University in Maryland. He became very famous for having separated Siamese twins joined at the back of the head in a 22-hour operation in Germany in 1987. His academic career and future political success, however, was set on course by a defining moment in the life of his mother.

Defining Moments Change Destinies

Two famous movies based on true stories highlight the power of defining moments. One was the Oscar award-winning® movie *Chariots of Fire*. In that movie, the character Eric Liddell has a defining moment when he refuses to run in the Olympics® on a Sunday. There have been many gold medal winners at the Olympic Games® over the decades, but few have inspired a movie decades after the event. The principled decision Liddell made in the face of huge global pressure became a defining moment for his life and inspired millions of people to stand for principle rather than buckle to public pressure. In a very similar vein, a more recent Mel Gibson movie, *Hacksaw Ridge*, documents the heroism of a Seventh Day Adventist soldier who refuses to carry a weapon into war. His defining moments happened as a child when he nearly killed his brother with a rock, and he saw his father nearly kill his mother with a gun. Those experiences defined for the rest of his life how he would respond to the carrying of weapons.

Getting back to Scripture, the Virgin Mary's visitation by the angel Gabriel described in Luke 1 was another clear defining moment. She set the course for life when she said *"Behold the maidservant of the LORD! Let it be to me according to your word."* Saul's decision (later Paul) to follow Christ on the road to Damascus was one of the Bible's most dramatic defining moments. Many times in later years, when speaking before kings and political leaders, he always referred back to that life-altering experience. When King Josiah in the Old Testament discovered the one copy left of the Holy

Scriptures in the temple, he made a defining moment covenant before God to implement the words he had read and the result was that he turned a whole nation back to God.

David changed his destiny and future when he made the decision to take on Goliath. Not only did he defeat the giant, but he gave the world an enduring image of how an underdog with God's help can overcome insurmountable odds. However, the direction and decisions of David were largely due to the supernatural anointing of God he experienced when Samuel was sent to anoint him as the next king while he was just a young shepherd boy in the presence of his father and brothers. A very important aspect of defining moments is when God, in a sovereign way, speaks a promise, a prophetic word or an inspired scripture into our lives. At the time we receive these, we need to test them before embracing them. When we know they are from God, they can provide a key defining moment for our lives because we can embark with surety in a certain direction.

Before I took my family for two years to be missionaries in Nigeria, I remember wrestling with the decision. At that time I was attending a godly church in Northern Virginia, and on a specific Sunday, I was at a communion service. The senior pastor was Rev. John Robert Topping, and he brought the communion recipients up to the altar in groups of about 25 at a time. After issuing the communion elements to the group he would normally pray a short blessing over the group and say something like "Go in peace and serve the LORD." When it came to my group, I remember being at the altar and praying this prayer "LORD, I will go to Nigeria but please just show me how." No sooner were the words out of my mouth, than Pastor Topping started to speak. Instead of his normal blessing and benediction, he spoke a word from God. "Many of you I have called," the LORD said, "but one of you I have called to take the light of my Gospel to a dark continent." From that point on, I never doubted my calling to do missionary work in Nigeria.

A defining moment for many of the disciples of Jesus was when, at His request, they made the choice to leave their lives as fishermen and to follow the carpenter from Nazareth. Abraham's decision to offer Isaac on an altar was another huge defining moment in the Bible. That single act of obedience changed the course of history, not only for the nation of Israel but for Christians around the world as God swore to offer His Son on the altar of the cross.

So defining moments do come in different forms, but essentially break down into four broad categories:

1) Events, understandings and decisions in our lives that establish values, principles, and patterns of behavior in us;

2) Events, understandings, and decisions that establish direction, goals and calling in us including promises and prophecies given by God to us;

3) Vows and commitments to people, to promises, to places and to purposes;

4) Decisions to take on responsibility for others, to have and raise a child, to take on a job or task or to pursue a long-term field of study. This can also include decisions to undertake major purchases and relational and financial covenants.

What's most important to understand concerning defining moments is the need to recognize them and for us to either undertake them prayerfully or respond to them with fidelity, faithfulness, and a good conscience. Let's not violate the foundational principles, relationships, callings, or promises that God has established in our lives because they are foundational to future maturity.

The Scripture given at the start of this chapter was 1 Corinthians 3:6, which Paul wrote: *"I (Paul) planted, Apollos watered, but GOD gave the increase."* It is very important to recognize that defining moments are the plantings of God in our lives. They are singular moments where divine seeds of future maturity are deposited. They are events that need to be followed by extensive processes, but they contain the DNA for future greatness.

So here is the principle of defining moments. When you make life-altering decisions, they normally happen at strategic God moments in your life. If properly followed through on, they can become strong pillars that help define your future. Your commitment to those decisions sets the sails of your boat and establishes the coordinates for your direction in life. The decision to pursue maturity is just one of those defining moments that will impact your destiny.

I want to conclude this section by sharing the words and the warning of the Apostle Paul to the young person Timothy that he was mentoring:

> "This charge I commit to you, son Timothy, according to the prophecies previously made concerning you, that by them you may wage the good warfare, having faith and a good conscience, which some having rejected, concerning the faith have suffered shipwreck."
> (1 Timothy 1:19 NKJV).

Rejecting faith and a good conscience can be very detrimental to our lives, and we can miss a defining moment that was meant to set us on the right course. To illustrate this warning I need to share one of the saddest letters that ever came to the church I attend, **The Rock Church and World Outreach Center** in San Bernardino, California. The founding pastors, Jim and Deborah Cobrae, are extremely close friends and I will talk about them later in this book. The church currently is pastored by Dan and Jessica Roth, has over 10,000 members and feeds over 500,000 people each year through their food distribution program. You will never leave a service at The Rock without being challenged to have a defining moment in your walk with God and to turn your life over to the Lordship of Jesus Christ. Here is what a young man by the name of Justin wrote some months after attending a service at The Rock:

"Dear Rock,

My name is Justin, I once went to your church. I sat in the back rows with the woman I loved, and she begged me to go up and get saved, I didn't. I felt it wasn't right at the time and a week later I ended up killing someone and got into a shootout with the police. Her biggest fear was that I would go to Hell since I didn't get saved.

I regret not getting saved that day. I regret being worried of what others would think of me walking down there in front of them. But now all I can think of is how life would have been different had I gotten saved, listened to the LORD, *and the woman I loved.*

Now I'm in a prison cell doing life, but I'll never forget your church and the day I turned down God. Now I'm saved, I dropped out of my gang and live to make others see what is right by living right. Please pray for me."

CHAPTER FIVE

The Maturing Process

*I planted, **Apollos watered**, but God gave the increase.*

— 1 Corinthians 3:6 NKJV

Defining moments are wonderful and life-changing, but they are singular events that MUST be followed by a maturing process. An event without a process to follow is like an arrow shot nowhere. Although I covered this quite extensively in my book, *Unlocking the Abraham Promise*, it still is worth mentioning afresh the PROCESS of maturing believers. Probably the greatest enemies to the maturing of Christian believers in the global Church are the event-oriented structures that exist in the Body of Christ.

In many local churches, we go from special service to special service, from seminar to camp to retreat to crusade to a special speaker. When we get done with one event, we immediately get a planning committee together to plan the next special outreach, concert or conference. It's not that events are evil, but alone they cannot get the job of life transformation done. This is because the kingdom of God in a person's life is not built on events but rather on process.

Let's look at the rest of society. Our education system is built on a systematic process as kids go through one grade to another and each subject is crafted to build on foundations laid in earlier grades. Our sports enterprises are built around starting youngsters at the earliest age in little leagues and gradually year-by-year developing their skill sets, their confidence, their competence, and their competitive experience. Our military and corporate structures likewise are built in the same way. It seems like only in the church do we expect a kind of biblical osmosis to take place. Even the traditional Sunday school structures that, in the past, provided some form of systematic scriptural instruction are being discarded by many churches for a more seeker-friendly organic type of approach.

Now I am not against being relevant and providing instruction in a dynamic manner but we should not be replacing milk with water and meat with milk and we should have a game plan to the process. Let's look at this principle in the Bible.

> "Whom will he teach knowledge? And whom will he make to understand the message? Those just weaned from milk? Those just drawn from the breasts? For precept must be upon precept, line upon line, here a little, there a little" (Isaiah 28:9 NKJV).

We cannot improve on this pattern. Instruction must be systematic, incremental, consistent, comprehensible, accurate, and must move believers towards mature understanding and fruitfulness. Most importantly the instruction of believers must be grounded in the Scriptures.

Some years ago, while actively involved in the missions work of a large local church, the children's pastor abruptly quit and left a huge void in the church's leadership. The senior pastor asked me if I would step in temporarily and take the helm until a replacement could be found. There were about 1,200 kids in the program with a large volunteer staff and a few paid co-workers. I was already a volunteer teacher in the program, so it seemed like a very manageable task. Nothing prepared me for the logistical nightmare that I faced.

The church at that time had a Saturday evening service and three Sunday morning services. They had a nursery, toddler, kinder and two elementary age groups. With their two elementary age groups, they insisted on moving the kids three or four times between classrooms during the 90 minutes they had them. Just keeping track of everything was a challenge. What was an even greater challenge was preparing teachers, curriculum and ministry time in a way that worked. I must admit that for my first six months I floundered in the job. It was then that I discovered the One Year® Bible and One Year® Devotional books from Tyndale. Each of these books had a single page Bible reading and a separate single page devotion reading based on the calendar dates of the year.

What these two books enabled me to do with a large children's church was amazing. I purchased cases of them and virtually forced every church family with elementary children to purchase a set. I then created a generous incentive program of Bible bucks, to encourage the parents to do a short daily Bible reading and devotional with their kids. They tracked their reading each week with a simple card, which the parents had to sign in order for the children to earn bucks on the weekend for their efforts. I hit up the parents for gifts and prizes to put in a store where the children could spend the Bible bucks and they generously obliged. I gave copies of the books to every teacher and now had seven Bible stories and seven devotions for them to teach from each week. On the weekend services, I did quizzes and games from their weekly readings and rewarded with money, prizes, and candy those who knew the previous week's content.

This one tool solved so many problems. I now had the kids going through a systematic overview of the Bible in a year from Genesis in January to Revelation in December.

I used animated and real-life videos each weekend to highlight the stories of the previous week drawing out of them valuable lessons and principles. Most importantly, I had a skeleton to build spiritual formation around in the kids, and I was now partnering with the parents to grow the faith of their youngsters instead of only getting them once a week.

Tyndale had three years of devotional books, so I kept the One Year® Bible each year with the 365 most strategic Bible stories, and I just changed the devotional book each year. Finally, I revamped the children's church rooms so I could fully control the lighting and media presentations. I had colorful Bible murals covering the walls, and I made the worship team from the main sanctuary come to our location after they had finished in the main service and lead the kids with quality worship. The kids were no secondary project, they got top quality treatment, and we saw the power of God move among them. Many would get caught up in worship, and nearly all of them got genuinely saved and filled with the Holy Spirit. God began to do great miracles in their lives.

There is nothing sacred about the specific plan that I used. The most important thing is that there MUST be a plan to disciple and build spiritual formation in young and old believers. In more recent years our ministry has developed a spiritual formation series for teenagers. It is a media-based curriculum called *YouthBytes* and our host Chad Daniel does possibly the craziest and most humorous presentation of biblical truth that I have ever encountered. We never compromise the message, but the method of presenting it is definitely up for grabs. The *YouthBytes* DVDs are flexible for use in just about any kind of meeting, and each episode comes with an icebreaker, a video and message summary, Scriptures, wild facts and figures about the episode's content, a complimentary written story and some group discussion questions. This lively program has helped hundreds of youth pastors to start laying spiritual formation in the lives of their young people.

In the New Testament, Paul refers to this systematic growth process as watering. In 1 Corinthians 3:6 he wrote, "*I planted, **Apollos watered**, but God gave the increase.*"

Taking this Scripture and examining it in parallel to the parable of the sower in Matthew 13, we see some interesting insights. The potential of the seed sown is said by Jesus to be 100 fold or a 10,000% increase of the original seed. The planting by Paul in 1 Corinthians 3:6 is the EVENT, or defining moment, which was obviously an evangelism endeavor where the Corinthian people found Christ as Savior. The watering by Apollos is the PROCESS that grows the seed to maturity and multiplication fruitfulness. From Acts 18 we understand more about Apollos and discover that he was *"mighty in the Scriptures"* and that he *"taught accurately"* the *"things of the LORD."* The process that brought forth increase of the original seed was accurate revelation teaching.

The revelation teaching of God's Word is the greatest instrument or vehicle of process that brings about the maturing of God's people. When I understood this, I began having a passion to gather the greatest revelation understandings I could find around the world, capture them on video and then translate them into as many languages as possible so that I could provide them to pastors, church leaders and individual believers anywhere and everywhere. I started with the foundational teaching of the ISOM, consisting of 160 teaching sessions by 30 very renowned instructors. I thought that was plenty, but God quickly showed me that it was just the foundation.

God challenged me with the life of Jesus. Here God in the flesh took over three years to live with and teach His disciples. If it took Jesus that long to get the original 11 discipled, then I felt I was not going to bypass the process of systematic discipleship. In the Great Commission Jesus says the following:

> And Jesus came and spoke to them, saying, "**All** authority has been given to Me in heaven and on earth. Go therefore and make disciples of **all** the nations, baptizing them in the name of the Father and of the Son and of the Holy Spirit, **teaching them to observe all things that I have commanded you**; and lo, I am with you **always**, even to the end of the age." (Matthew 28:18-20 NKJV).

The superlative nature of this command is staggering. FOUR times Jesus uses the word ALL. He says ALL authority is backing the making of disciples process, and the scope of the task is ALL nations. The PROCESS is *"teaching them to observe all things that I have commanded you,"* and the promise carries with it the assurance that if we undertake this task, He will be with us ALWAYS.

If every person reading this could get a hold of this understanding, that PROCESS matures people in their Christian faith, and that REVELATION TEACHING is the vehicle God uses to facilitate that process, we would finally be able to fulfill Christ's Great Commission. This is why I am tirelessly passionate about developing vehicles of process to help LOCAL CHURCHES to systematically train people in the word of God.

We developed the ISOM (160 sessions of revelation teaching), then *YouthBytes* (a full year of teen curriculum), then Women of the World (a year of training for God's ladies), then a Bachelors program (another 160 sessions of revelation teaching), and then a Masters program (another 96 sessions of teaching). This is in addition to 52 sessions in a Community Development program and additional training for Marketplace ministry. These are just some of the tools we have created to help facilitate the maturing of God's people around the world. The original recordings of all these teachings are one thing, but translating their voice and notes is an additional task that is often expensive, difficult and time-consuming. We do that work tirelessly because it is the way to get the job done in the harvest fields of the world. We find that it is SO appreciated in foreign language countries and especially in persecuted nations.

It's not any specific teaching that does the task, but whenever individuals or local churches embrace vehicles of process that contain revelation teaching about a specific subject, their people will grow and mature in whatever area they teach on. Events and defining moments are wonderful but whenever you have an event, think through the VEHICLE OF PROCESS that you will use to mature the believers following the event.

Entrusted with Other People
What is the driving motivation behind these VEHICLES OF PROCESS, it is PEOPLE. Jesus said these words at the Last Supper in his prayer to the Father in John 17:12 NKJV:

> "[. . .] Those whom you gave me, I have kept; and none of them is lost except the son of perdition, that the Scripture might be fulfilled."

Both Jesus and the Apostle Paul were not only concerned with finishing their own races well, but both realized that they also had been entrusted with the development of others. Although Jesus prayed all night before choosing the 12 key people He would mentor, He still refers to them as *"those whom You (the Father) gave me."* I believe there are certain people in this world that God is entrusting us to keep. Jesus says, *"I have kept,"* meaning He took personal responsibility for the protection and development of those people.

The Apostle Paul recognized that at the judgment seat of Christ, he not only had to present himself but also the other believers with whom God had entrusted him.

> For I am jealous over you with godly jealousy: for I have espoused you to one husband, that I may present you as a chaste virgin to Christ (2 Corinthians 11:2 KJV).

Suzanna Wesley

> "The hand that rocks the cradle is the hand that rules the world."
>
> — William Wallace

Any person who is a parent will know well this sense of responsibility and this weight of nurture. Suzanna Wesley was the 25th child in a family of 25 kids. Her son John Wesley was the 16th child out of 19. Here is what Suzanna wrote about her task of mentoring her many children:

> "Though the education of so many children must create an abundance of trouble, and will perpetually keep the mind employed as well as the body; yet I consider it no small honor to be entrusted with the care of so many souls. And if that trust be but managed with prudence and integrity, the harvest will abundantly recompense the toil of the seed-time; and it will be certainly no little inheritance to the future glory to stand forth at the last day and say, "LORD, here are the children which Thou hast given me, of whom I have lost none by my ill example, nor by neglecting to instill into their minds, in their early years, the principles of Thy true religion and virtue!"

John Wesley preached 10,000 sermons and traveled 80,000 miles on horseback. He so impacted his generation that history credits his influence for stopping England from having a bloody revolution the way that France had. A huge amount of credit needs to go to a mother who took the task of mentoring her son to maturity seriously. One of her other sons, Charles Wesley, wrote 6,500 hymns and was a key leader in the Methodist movement in Great Britain.

Converts versus Disciples

The modern-day preoccupation of the Church seems to revolve largely around converts, which is the event without the process to follow. An honest reading of the New Testament puts the emphasis of salvation on finishing the race of faith, not just starting it. Consider these Scriptures:

> But he who endures to the end shall be saved (Matthew 24:13 NKJV).
>
> But I keep under my body, and bring it into subjection: lest that by any means, when I have preached to others, I myself should be a castaway (1 Corinthians 9:27 KJV).
>
> Not that I have already attained, or am already perfected; but I press on, that I may lay hold of that for which Christ Jesus has also laid hold of me. Brethren, I do not count myself to have apprehended; but one thing I do, forgetting those things which are behind and reaching forward to those things which are ahead, I press toward the goal for the prize of the upward call of God in Christ Jesus (Philippians 3:12-14 NKJV).
>
> Receiving the end of your faith—the salvation of your souls (1 Peter 1:9 NKJV).

Paul considered embracing a faith in Christ to be only a birth. Just as growth to maturity in real life is the normal, natural and expected process, so it MUST be in the spiritual realm. Peter says the end of your faith produces the salvation of your soul so we must bring people to the end of their faith and not focus so entirely on the beginning. In today's church, we seem to have so many people who are stuck in an arrested state of development or in a teenage adolescence. It seems like very few believers develop the massive potential of *"[. . .] Christ in you, the hope of glory."* (Colossians 1:27 NKJV).

It was the realization of that potential in the early church that enabled them to *"turn their world upside down."* It is still an awesome feat that without modern means of communication, no cell phones or Internet, no airplanes, cars or trains, the early church was able to impact its generation so incredibly. It's been said about the early church:

> "If they did what they did with what they had, imagine what we could do with what we have if we had what they had."
>
> — Source unknown

The Early Church had mature believers who were fearless in their faith and who demonstrated to their world the power of God and the life of Christ. As we move into these end times, I believe that Christ wants to restore that maturity of faith to

His Bride. We must learn to mentor believers to maturity and we must not just be interested in EVENTS but also in the PROCESS to follow that will facilitate people growing to maturity.

Women of the World
Three quick examples before I close this chapter. Back in 2005, we launched our Women of the World (WOW) curriculum at the Cuneta Astrodome in Metro-Manila in the Philippines. My wife Lisa had spearheaded that project from its outset and, during the conference, got to meet with Gloria Arroyo, the President at that time of the Philippines. There was a group in the Presidential Palace using our WOW program, and we found that it was also being used in a prison nearby. So from the prison to the palace, women were being blessed by the WOW program. Many thousands of ladies packed out that wonderful venue as they listened to great women teachers such as Bobbie Houston, Lisa Bevere, Deborah Cobrae, my wife Lisa and many others. When we left the Philippines, we felt that a solid launching event had taken place to that WOW product but, as we looked back, we saw some real mistakes. We had focused too much on the event and not enough on the process to follow.

So in 2006, we decided to have another launching event for WOW in the heart of Europe. We consciously decided to make that event even more effective than the Philippines launch. This time we chose a venue in Germany that held over 1,000 people but then, via satellite, we had about 110 additional gatherings of believers in churches in five European nations tuning into the conference and launch. More than 10,000 people were in this way able to participate at a very reasonable cost. We made everything bilingual in English and German and the speakers participating were outstanding. We also decided that, although WOW was a women's program, that we should add men into the equation and so our speakers included John and Lisa Bevere, John and Helen Burns, Joyce Meyer, Darlene Zschech, Christine Caine, Deborah Cobrae and Lisa and I. There were three solid husband and wife couples ministering alongside each other.

The theme of the Germany conference was "Men and Women—Side by Side." Adding in the men made the conference so much more effective because we were able to challenge the paradigms in the hearts of European pastors and leaders. Lisa and I did a message on Queen Esther, showing how God put the salvation of the entire Jewish people, including the line of the Messiah, firmly on the shoulders of a woman. She, however, had to partner with Mordecai and had to function under the spiritual covering of her husband. I challenged the male leadership across Europe to reach out the scepter, like the husband of Esther had, to enable the callings of godly women in their churches.

The inclusion of the men brought about a significant breakthrough at the Germany conference, but it was the process that followed that truly made the additional difference. Whereas in Manila we had focused mostly on the EVENT of the conference, in Germany we focused both on the event and the PROCESS that followed. Not only did we sell tens of thousands of Euros worth of product during and after the event, but we were able to start close to 1,000 groups of ladies who took the WOW teachings in small groups for a period of six months to a year following the event. I learned a HUGE lesson. Use EVENTS to *ignite* the PROCESS to follow.

Saltillo in Mexico

This brings me to the second example, which happened more recently. Less than two summers ago, I was invited to do a graduation in Minnesota at a small Spanish speaking church. Of their roughly 160 members, over half were enrolled in ISOM, and the church was alive with God's power and presence. As I was there for the weekend, the leadership of the church requested a special closed-door meeting at 4 PM on a Saturday afternoon. I was not prepared for what I was going to face.

In the meeting, I sat with about 20 leaders from the church, and they told me what had just happened during the past year down in Mexico. For about the seven previous years, they said, they had been traveling to a small town by the name of Saltillo in Mexico near Monterrey. Each year they had followed a similar pattern of ministering in the churches, taking food, clothing and practical gifts to bless the believers in that city. Each following year they would return, and things were pretty much the same as the previous year, and they would repeat the pattern.

All that changed, however, in 2016, when another English speaking church purchased a license for the ISOM for their church. It was a modest $1,900 investment but was a generous and strategic missions-minded action. This license allowed them the legal ability to start as many Bible schools in Mexico as they wanted. So when they went down that 2016 year, they launched about 23 ISOM schools and began training over 300 students. They were not prepared for the transformation and change that took place. When they returned the following year, expecting the same as the previous seven years, they discovered hundreds of students on fire for God. One church had to move location twice in the past year because they kept outgrowing their facility. Miracles were happening in the lives of the believers, and evangelism was taking place into nearby and remote villages.

The reason these 20 leaders cornered me in Minnesota was to ask my advice as to how to deal with the explosion of growth and demand that introducing the ISOM had created. They were literally awed and scared by what was taking place. The following year they graduated 43 students, and over 70 were scheduled to graduate in the year following that. These newly trained believers were now mature enough to step into ministry functions, and they were on fire to win their region for God. The only difference between the other seven times they had visited Saltillo was they introduced a PROCESS to follow their yearly visiting EVENT.

Romania after the fall of the Nicolae Ceausescu Regime

On Christmas Day of 1989, the dictators of Romania, Nicolae and his wife Elena Ceausescu were tried and executed by a firing squad on the same day. A new wave of freedom for the Gospel began to sweep through the nation and doors opened for Christian ministries to work and do outreach in the country. In 1990 and 1991, Evangelist Luis Palau spent 20 days in Romania at the invitation of the newly established Evangelical Alliance of Romania. Taking place just weeks after the fall of the Communist Regime, these campaigns brought together more than 340,000 people to hear the Gospel, with more than 85,600 individuals making public commitments to Jesus Christ.

Now at that time in Romania, because of the brutal communist regime that had ruled the country for decades, Romanian language Bibles were extremely rare and were greatly treasured by believers. During those two campaigns in 1990 and 1991, Christian believers from the West had made the decision to donate a large number of Bibles to those in Romania who made decisions for Christ during the campaigns.

Initially, the idea was to hand out the Bibles to the new converts at the point of their decision for Christ, right after the altar call at the front of the podium. But then someone who was thinking through the process to follow made a different suggestion. Why not hand all the new converts a map of the city showing all the participating churches. Then have every church run new believer classes for six evenings following the campaign. If they completed a new believer class at one of those churches, then they would get a brand new Bible.

Simply by moving the giving of a Bible from after the sinner's prayer to after the new believers class caused thousands of new converts to join new churches. After they had attended six meetings in one of them, they felt loved and comfortable enough to join the church. It was one of the most successful campaigns Luis Palau ever had because somebody thought through the process and not just the event.

CHAPTER 5: THE MATURING PROCESS

I have given examples of a major conference, of a missions trip and of a Gospel crusade. I am only trying to provoke ideas concerning how events can be maximized by using them to ignite a process to follow. Just think how many thousands of Christian endeavors consist of EVENTS without a PROCESS. This happens all the time at camps, crusades, seminars, mission trips, plays, outreach days and many other well-meaning Christian endeavors. The lesson from this chapter is to always think through the PROCESS that will lead to maturity and ask God how to use EVENTS to *ignite* an ongoing maturing PROCESS.

CHAPTER SIX

Maturity and Identity

> "The most important human endeavor is the striving for morality in our actions. Our inner balance and even our very existence depend on it. Only morality in our actions can give beauty and dignity to life. To make this a living force and bring it to clear consciousness is perhaps the foremost task of education."
>
> — Albert Einstein

One of the most classic movie stories of our day is that of *The Lion King*. Despite its fictional base, this story has much to teach in the areas of identity and of one's ability to fulfill destiny in a mature way. I contend that it's virtually impossible for a person to walk in maturity if their sense of self-worth has been shattered, most often by a lie, but also frequently by a personal violation of ethics.

Many famous people have had their careers destroyed because of serious ethical violations in their personal lives. Those are often self-inflicted wounds, but in the case of *The Lion King*, it is the influence of a malevolent enemy and the believing of a lie that opened the door to defeat.

The Lion King begins with a glorious scene full of high promise at the birth of Simba, the future king of the beasts. There is an air of celebration with the arrival of Simba, and the atmosphere is pregnant with the prospect of a new heir to the lion throne and of continued blessing and prosperity in the lion kingdom under the wise rulership of Mufasa.

In the lion's kingdom, there is also, however, the ever-lurking presence of wicked Scar, a great depiction of the devil with his hyena friends who represent demonic and devious entities in the kingdom.

As the movie progresses, Scar orchestrates a stampede with the clear goal of killing both Mufasa and Simba. Only Mufasa is murdered, and Simba is left devastated. Scar immediately convinces Simba that the death of his father is his fault. Simba believes the lie and becomes guilt-ridden. This leaves him full of condemnation and defeat. He leaves the lion kingdom to try and escape his shame and grows up physically in a foreign land.

This leaves a vacuum of leadership in the lion kingdom, which Scar readily fills. Scar takes over the kingdom, and it quickly deteriorates into a devastated wasteland under his cruel and wicked rule.

In the foreign land, where Simba is growing physically to full maturity, he has a visitation from his father. He makes the decision, despite his guilt and shame, to return to the kingdom to try and take it back. Upon his tepid return, Scar immediately attacks Simba and pins him down, ready to destroy him once and for all.

It is at this point that Scar makes a serious mistake and, out of malicious glee, reveals the truth to Simba. He confesses to having orchestrated the death of Mufasa and reveals his contempt for the hyenas who have been helping him. The hyenas overhear the confession and become outraged, but the biggest identity transformation takes place in Simba.

As soon as the truth that he is not guilty of his father's death enters the heart of Simba, so does courage and strength. He rises up with boldness and power, overcomes Scar, and throws him down to be devoured by the, now disgusted, waiting hyenas.

Simba takes the reigns of the lion kingdom and peace and prosperity return. The devastated wasteland transforms magically into a green oasis of blessing. The kingdom is firmly established under the hand of Simba, and he takes a place of MATURE leadership, thus fulfilling his destiny.

So many young people today are confused about their identity. They are confused about their faith, their purpose in life, their gender, and their origins. Satan plays on their fears and, like with Simba, does everything he can to lie to them, heap on guilt and condemnation and try to prevent them from discovering their true identity and entering into their destiny.

We have to help young people understand that they are created in the image of God, that they are whom God says they are and that they have been redeemed with the highest price Heaven can pay, the blood of Jesus Christ. They also need to understand that they were created for a purpose and that God has a divine destiny on their lives. As the Apostle Paul prayed in Ephesians for EVERY believer, that *"they may know the hope of their calling."* Only with a good and a God identity can young people truly enter into the full maturity of their calling.

In order for a person to have a healthy sense of self-worth, they need to have a solid understanding of their origins (where they came from). A right foundational perspective of origins will enable a person to grasp who they are in the present (their correct identity) and where they are going (their purpose).

All these areas have been under huge assault, and it's no wonder that many young people today suffer from depression. It also helps explain why teen suicide is at an all-time high. ORIGINS are at the root of everything, and it's that topic that I want to confront squarely.

Origins
The huge battle to control the high ground in America's schools with regards to origins and evolution is really a battle over controlling who defines identity.

If human beings are just a product of random chance and no divine spark gave rise to life, then there is little incentive to follow any moral code and little purpose to existence. The value of life becomes quite meaningless, and this worldview can only lead to selfish and often destructive behavior.

What a person believes about their origins has a huge bearing on their behavior, their actions and how they function in society. The attack against a God-based worldview of our origins has primarily come from science and academia. In many ways, however, the study of science, and especially of DNA should actually help establish and strengthen people's faith in God and in His design in creation. Let's look at DNA first.

DNA
I read a few years ago about one of the world's most renowned atheists Dr. Antony Flew (1923–2010). Flew was a British professor who taught at Oxford University in the area of philosophy of religion. At the age of 81, he changed from being an atheist to believing in God based primarily on DNA research and scientific discovery. Flew ended up writing a book titled *There is NO God* but the NO was crossed out, and an *A* replaced it, so it was really titled *There is A God*.

Flew wrote in 2004, "My one and only piece of relevant evidence for God is the apparent impossibility of providing a naturalistic theory of the origins from DNA of the first reproducing species..." "[In fact], the only reason which I have for beginning to think of believing in a First Cause [God], is the impossibility of providing a naturalistic account of the origin of the first reproducing organisms." In 2006, Flew joined 11 other academics in urging the British government to teach intelligent design in the state schools.

In 2007, in an interview with Benjamin Wiker, Flew said again that his deism was the result of his "growing empathy with the insight of Einstein and other noted scientists that there had to be an intelligence behind the integrated complexity of the physical Universe" and his "own insight that the integrated complexity of life itself, which is far more complex than the physical universe, can only be explained in terms of an Intelligent Source."

An honest look at a few DNA facts should give all thinking people some doubts about the universe existing without God through random chance. It also will give every person a glimpse into their own true origins and makeup. On average, an adult human body has 37 trillion cells in it. What's most important to understand is that EVERY person starts off as ONE single cell called a zygote. That cell is microscopic and barely visible to the human eye. Contained in this microscopic speck is the incredibly complex code that will determine virtually every aspect of a person's life.

If you uncoiled the DNA in one cell, it would be about 5 feet long. If you stretched out the DNA in ONE human body end to end, it would reach from the earth to the sun and back over 500 times.

Each of the 37 trillion cells in the human body, including that first one, has a nucleus with 46 chromosomes (23 pairs), which contain a person's DNA and genes. The DNA is coiled like a mass of spaghetti inside the chromosomes.

This DNA code contains a blueprint stretching back into every ancestor of a person's history, all the way back to the first human that existed on the planet and the information in that ONE cell will determine the intricate makeup of those yet to be born through the lineage of that individual.

At the Molecular Level
Scientists tell us that every human being spent about a half an hour as a single cell so let's briefly examine the very first cell that each of us originally was.

Conception itself is a mind-boggling miracle. The way that billions of pieces of information from two distinct and different human beings can seamlessly merge and form the basis for a new, completely independent different person is almost impossible to explain and even more difficult to comprehend. We all need to honestly think of the intelligence that must govern the creation of a human life from the joined cells of two separate human beings, the process of sexual intimacy that brings that about and the total integration of two human histories into a new creation. Consider for a moment the microscopic processes in that NEW one single cell.

This one zygote cell has its own identity, its own unique DNA structure and its potential is absolutely staggering. This single zygote cell contains the ability to build a human brain capable of storing not only vast amounts of information but also of carrying human intelligence, consciousness, thoughts, ideas, dreams, visions and purpose. Even more profound is that ONE microscopic cell's ability to create emotion, conscience, perception, relationship, spirituality, and intimacy.

That single microscopic cell contains the governing instructions of billions of integrated human functions spanning the whole of a person's life. The code encapsulates life itself, something no laboratory has ever been able to replicate.

We are now zooming in and examining roughly five feet of DNA in the ONE cell that we all were for the first half hour of our lives. Each piece of DNA in that original ONE cell consists of two strands that are held together in the shape of a double helix. The huge double helix molecule is built as a long string of nucleotides. There are four kinds of nucleotides in the construction: adenine, thymine, cytosine, and guanine. I know this may bring many of you back to painful memories of high school biology but stay with me as we try to unpack this microscopic miracle.

These nucleotides, when in a double DNA helix, are called base PAIRS because adenine always pairs with thymine and cytosine always pairs with guanine. Each human cell has about 3 BILLION base pairs, and these provide the coding for a person's whole body and entire life. Scientists call this DNA structure in ONE cell the human genome.

The human genome is so complex that it took scientists almost 13 years to map it out and cost over 3 billion dollars. There were 20 lab centers working together in six countries and dozens of scientists in each lab. Some of the world's fastest supercomputers were used to map up to 40 million base pairs each day. This whole undertaking was called the "Human Genome Project."

Okay, let's step back and look at this. Mapping out the code contained in ONE microscopic human cell took hundreds of scientists 13 years working together worldwide in 20 laboratories using supercomputers, and they barely scratched the surface in understanding it. Just the UK lab had 87 scientists engaged in this one single project.

When the genome code of ONE cell was finally cracked, there was an announcement on June 26, 2000, in the East Room of the White House, where President Bill Clinton had this to say:

> "Today, we are learning the language in which God created life. We are gaining ever more awe for the complexity, the beauty, and the wonder of God's most divine and sacred gift."

Francis Collins, the National Medal of Science winning head of the Human Genome Project, added this:

> "It's a happy day for the world. It is humbling for me, and awe-inspiring, to realize that we have caught the first glimpse of our own instruction book, previously known only to God."

That genome script and sequence is three billion letters long written in that strange and cryptographic four-letter code that I have already described. If that code were to be printed out in a book form, the pages would stack as high as the Washington Monument, which is 555 feet tall. That's simply the instruction manual contained in ONE human cell.

These DNA strands are not small entities. Just the first chromosome which scientists call Chromosome 1 has 249 million base pairs. These base pairs are in a very specific sequence, and that sequence reveals the blueprint of about 25,000 genes. A gene is simply the sequence of coding found in one side of a piece of the DNA helix and then only a small section of the strand. The length of each gene ranges from 27,000 nucleotides to a sequence of over two million nucleotides. Just on Chromosome 1 is found the coding for more than 2,000 genes.

As you will understand in a moment, the genes coded into the 46 chromosomes are the blueprints to create millions of proteins. The complexity here is astonishing. Each cell is like a massively complex miniature factory. The DNA is located inside the nucleus, surrounded by a nuclear membrane. The nucleus is only about 10% of the cell's volume, and it floats in a substance that biologists call cytoplasm.

If your naked eye can barely see a single human cell, it most definitely cannot see the nucleus, which is a tenth of the size, without a good microscope. It's inside that tenth of a single cell that ALL the coding for a human life, past, present, and future, can be found. ALL the 46 chromosomes containing that information are located inside the nucleus.

What enables the information from the DNA to get used by the cell involves another entity called a messenger RNA. This single-stranded structure literally "reads" the coding on one of the genes found on one side of the DNA helix and then escapes through a hole in the nuclear plasma wall out into the cytoplasm of the cell. There it finds another micro entity called a ribosome.

Floating around in the cytoplasm of the cell are about 20 different amino acids just waiting to be used. Using the code from a DNA gene as a blueprint, the ribosome reads three nucleotides at a time from the messenger RNA and, based on a predetermined pattern, and it assigns an amino acid into a building sequence on the other side of the ribosome. When the sequence is completed, the amino acids FOLD in an extremely intricate way, into a very specific protein cell. If one nucleotide is out of sequence, the protein won't work.

These are mind-boggling complex structures, and billions of these structures are being created in our bodies every day. In this way, a ribosome will create lung cells, heart cells, eye cells and every specific cell for the human body. Now from those 25,000 genes coded into the DNA strands, the human body is able to create about two million different kinds of proteins. About 55,000 of those proteins are enzymes. What's scary to know is that if your body is missing just ONE enzyme out of 55,000, you die.

Now please don't let some of these figures cause your eyes to glaze over. Think deeply about it, there are 55,000 enzyme catalysts all simultaneously coordinating and facilitating chemical reactions in your body right now, and if just ONE enzyme were to be missing or fail, you would die.

The code in the DNA contains such detail, such wisdom, such intricate intelligence that it's difficult even to begin to wrap your brain around it. Not only does this code have to initiate the formation of other cells, but it has to deliberately develop, in an incredibly complex sequence, systems and structures and entities like the eye, the brain, the liver, the kidneys, the heart, the skeletal structure, and the reproductive systems, just to name a few.

How does that ONE microscopic cell know how to set the heart rate, the temperature of the body, the communication systems, the delivery of nutrition systems, the elimination of waste systems and the coordinated growth systems of all 37 trillion cells in the body? Remember that every cell has to be nurtured, fed, coordinated, integrated and supported every moment of every day throughout a lifetime. Consider some of these facts:

- A normal adult human body has about 60,000 miles of blood vessels. Placed end-to-end they would stretch more than twice around the earth.
- The surface area of human lungs is equal to the size of a tennis court.
- Impulses from the brain travel at 170 miles per hour.
- A person's liver performs over 500 different functions.
- A person's nose can remember about 50,000 different scents, and a human body at adulthood has 206 different bones.
- Just to take one step, a person will use about 200 different muscles.
- A human eye can distinguish about 10 million different colors.
- During a lifetime, a human heart will pump about 1.5 million barrels of blood.
- Each human kidney contains one million filters that clean about 1.3 liters of blood every minute and push out about 1.5 liters of urine daily.

If this very simple scientific summary I have given does not give you some sense of awe, then I'm not sure what will accomplish that. Think of what we are teaching our children, that everything I have described happened by random chance and that we are all the result of some kind of accident. That, my friend, takes a LOT more faith than believing in God.

Getting back to the earlier part of this chapter, these types of facts I have outlined is why one of the world's most famous atheists, Dr. Antony Flew, began to believe in God at the age of 81. I again quote what he wrote, and this time it will make much more sense: "My one and only piece of relevant evidence for God is the apparent impossibility of providing a naturalistic theory of the origins from DNA of the first reproducing species . . ." "[In fact], the only reason which I have for beginning to think of believing in a First Cause [God], is the impossibility of providing a naturalistic account of the origin of the first reproducing organisms."

Again in the interview with Benjamin Wiker, he said that he had a "growing empathy with the insight of Einstein and other noted scientists that there had to be an intelligence behind the integrated complexity of the physical universe" and his "own insight that the integrated complexity of life itself, which is far more complex than the physical universe, can only be explained in terms of an Intelligent Source."

What I have shared so far are just a few amazing facts about the human body, which, most of the time, we take for granted. The point I'm trying to drive at is that each human being, no matter how poor their self-image, is a miraculous creation. Hopefully, we can reach the point King David did where we exclaim: *"I'm fearfully and wonderfully made"* (Psalms 139:24 NKJV).

When you realize that your identity is rooted in the fact that you are created in the image of God, that you are NOT an accident but rather a miracle, that's a beginning point at which you can start looking to Him for meaning, understanding, and identity.

When a candidate runs to become the President of the United States and successfully gets elected, they initially seem quite awkward when they step into the actual office of the presidency. What then happens is quite remarkable; they embrace the presidential identity, they believe it is theirs to walk in, and over a very short period of time they start to walk, talk and act 'presidential.' You have to believe an identity, embrace it, and then you will actually become it.

I believe the same thing happens with us when we embrace God's identity for us. We are His children, and we are created in His image. It's not about our thoughts, our feelings or our emotions. When we embrace His identity for us, confusion will start to leave, and we will begin to walk in His truth. Quite literally, His truth about ourselves will set us free from self-doubt, confusion and a lack of self-worth. Simply put, a mature identity is a God-based identity.

This principle of discovering God's divinely revealed truth about everything in life, believing it, embracing it, and learning to walk in it, is a key to becoming a mature man or woman of God.

The Age of the Universe
DNA is not the only hurdle to understand in order to embrace a God-based biblical worldview. Actually, just believing that the Bible is the inspired Word of God is difficult for many to embrace. One of the biggest obstacles to people accepting the Bible as TRUTH is found in the very first chapter of Genesis. The issue of whether the Bible or science has it correct when it comes to the age of the universe is a big hurdle for people to cross. If you can't believe in Genesis 1, how is it possible to believe in John 3 that speaks about God sending Jesus to save us from our sins?

I want to start with my own journey in these areas. After my ministry had recorded many world experts in the areas of Bible instruction, women's issues, community development, sexuality, money, and marketplace engagement, I realized that we also needed to tackle the apparent chasm between Scripture and science in the Genesis 1 creation story.

Like with all other topics, we searched around the world for a profoundly qualified expert who could clearly articulate an academically believable explanation of their understanding of this difficult topic. We settled on Dr. Gerald Schroeder, a physicist with a double Ph.D. from MIT and a renowned Hebrew scholar. Dr. Schroeder is one of Israel's leading scientists and mentions in the introduction of his book *The Science of God: The Convergence of Scientific and Biblical Wisdom*, that he has observed six atomic weapons being tested, convincing him that human beings NEED to work for peace seriously.

We had to fly Dr. Schroeder from his home in Jerusalem to Los Angeles to record with us on this Genesis 1 topic, and his perspective was both fascinating and extremely convincing.

Schroeder explained that both science and Scripture start with a Big Bang, an ignition point that still today gives us an expanding universe. That huge explosion is as far back as science takes us, so it's also a good place to start Scripturally. It's the opening verse of the Bible, "In the beginning, God created the heavens and the earth." It's a huge point of agreement that both science and Scripture agree that there was actually "a beginning."

Now, according to Schroeder, it's important to understand that Hebrew scholarship has never argued for the six days of Genesis to be measured as six rotations of the earth but rather six 24-hour periods. After all, he points out, the sun and moon are only created on the fourth day (Genesis 1:14–18) so earth rotations cannot be the measure. So in Genesis 1, we are dealing with real time, not earth rotation time. In Schroeder's own words:

> "There is a simple answer to the problem of a scientifically old and biblically young universe, an answer that has within it the core of a complex truth. Time as described in the Bible may not be the same as we know time today. We find a hint for this in the 2,900-year-old Book of Psalms: 'A thousand years in Your sight are as a day that passes, as a watch in the night' (Ps. 90:4) Perhaps from a biblical perspective the six days of Genesis include the fifteen billion years we earthbound mortals estimate to be the span of time since the beginning of time, just as a watch in the night might include a thousand years."
> (Science of God, 44)

Schroeder says the evidence for this understanding is contained in the Hebrew language used when it comes to documenting the six days. Each day ends with a statement similar to verse 23 of Genesis 1, *"So the evening and the morning were the fifth day."*

Every day's ending in Genesis 1 is similar in construct to this sentence except the FIRST day. According to Schroeder the first day in the Hebrew states *"So the evening and the morning, DAY 1."* This, he says, is because the time in the narrative is unfolding from the point of the Big Bang going forward and, at that point, no day had ever existed so it was simply setting a marker and reference point from which all future days in the universe would be measured.

So the second through sixth days were able to use that first-day standard and have a reference point but not DAY ONE. DAY ONE is the reference point. This is clear evidence, according to Schroeder, that the time of the six days in Genesis 1 is unfolding forwards and needs to be analyzed from the point of the Big Bang going forward, not from a Mount Sinai perspective looking backward. According to Schroeder, there is a clear switch in the Hebrew language to current earth time when the narrative moves into Chapter 2 and the Garden of Eden story.

Time According to Einstein
Schroeder comes at this issue of time from a number of different perspectives. Probably most helpful is the great scientist Albert Einstein's 1915 scientific paper revealing a concept called the theory of relativity. This showed that the rate of the passage of time was relative to energy, mass, gravity, and velocity or in equation form $E=mc^2$.

This theory has now been verified thousands of times and is now called the "Law of Relativity." What this means is that time on the earth will pass slower than time on the moon and faster than time on the sun. This is because the gravity on the moon is less and the gravity on the sun is more.

Schroeder points out something that is easier for us to grasp and that is weight. We can weigh 150 pounds here on earth, but if we traveled to the moon and took out our scale, we would only be 25 pounds up there. That is because gravity is that much less on the moon. (Science of God, 50)

Time is relative, and just that very concept is difficult for anybody to grasp. Most people have a tough time understanding Einstein's theory of relativity, where time is dependent on velocity, mass, gravity, and energy. If a person were able to travel at the speed of light (186,000 miles per second), then time would literally stand still. A fascinating thing that Schroeder writes is:

> "Visible light rays, invisible microwaves, X rays, and gamma rays are all forms of the same type of radiant energy known as electromagnetic radiation. As science has discovered, radiant energy does not experience the flow of time. Radiant energy, such as the light rays you are seeing at this very moment, exists in a state that might be described as an "eternal now," a state in which time does not pass. (This is a concept we can write but not intellectually grasp because all our existence is within the flow of time.)" (Science of God, 58)

We know from Scripture that God is light and that is possibly one reason that God exists outside of time and space and that He can be the beginning and the end at the same time. He is the great I AM, always existent in the present. With God, there is NO TIME.

The Six Days of Genesis
Because time is relative to speed and gravity, the universe would have been expanding rapidly at close to the speed of light during that first day and time would have been unfolding extremely slowly. That first day would be about 8 billion earth years in today's time but only 24 hours then. Anyone with training in physics and with an understanding of Einstein's theory of relativity and $E=mc^2$ will understand this reasoning.

According to Schroeder, as the universe expanded, it slowed in its rate of expansion, following a formula of a half-life each day. He gives a lot of scientific reasons for this, which are outlined in his book *The Science of God*. Part of it has to do with matter moving rapidly apart on both sides of a center point thus doubling the distance between the expanding matter. As he puts it "Each doubling in size 'slowed' the cosmic clock by a factor of 2."

With Schroeder being a double Ph.D. physicist from MIT, I don't think I'm in a scientific position to argue with him, but intuitively it does make sense. We know today the rate of expansion of the universe and know that over the vast expanses of time there has been a slowing. Schroeder makes a compelling case that each day of expansion is a half-life of the previous day. So day 1 was 8 billion years, day 2 was 4 billion years, day 3 was 2 billion years, day 4 was 1 billion years, day 5 was 500 million years and day six is in progress being about 250,000 million years. This puts us very close to what scientists say is the age of the universe. It was both six 24-hour days and 15.75 billion years.

What's even more intriguing is that these designations closely match the fossil record and the days outlined in Genesis 1 are directly in cohesion with science (The Science of God, 70).

Day 1 (first 8 billion years) – **the Bible says** the creation of the universe; light separates from dark (Gen. 1:1–5).
Day 1 (first 8 billion years) – **Science says** the Big Bang marks the creation of the universe; light literally breaks free as electrons and bond to atomic nuclei; galaxies start to form.

Day 2 (next 4 billion years) – **The Bible says** the heavenly firmament forms (Gen. 1:6–8).
Day 2 (next 4 billion years) – **Science says** the disk of the Milky Way forms; Sun, a main sequence star, forms.

Day 3 (next 2 billion years) – **The Bible says** oceans and dry land appear; the first life, plants, appear (Gen. 1:9–13).
Day 3 (next 2 billion years) – **Science says** the earth had cooled by this time and large bodies of water appear 3.8 billion years ago followed almost immediately by first forms of life: bacteria and photosynthetic algae appear.

Day 4 (next 1 billion years) – **The Bible says** the Sun, Moon, and stars become visible in the heavens (Gen. 1:14-19).
Day 4 (next 1 billion years) – **Science says** the Earth's atmosphere becomes transparent; photosynthesis produces an oxygen-rich atmosphere.

Day 5 (next 500 million years) – **The Bible says** first animal life swarms abundantly in waters; followed by reptiles and winged animals (Gen. 1:20-23).
Day 5 (next 500 million years) – **Science says** that the first multicellular animals appear; waters swarmed with animal life having the basic body plans of all future animals; winged insects appear.

Day 6 (next 250 million years) – **The Bible says** that land animals, mammals, and humankind appear (Gen. 1:24-31).
Day 6 (next 250 million years) – **Science says** massive extinction destroys over 90% of life. The land is repopulated; hominids and then humans appear.

Light being the Clock of the Universe

Schroeder does not only come at the age of the universe from an Einstein perspective, but also from the clues that light in the universe reveals to us. This is because scientists have discovered that light generated by a star sends to us it's timing in the waves of light it sends us. Schroeder says it like this:

> "The clock of the universe is the light of the universe. Each wave of light is a tick of the cosmic clock. The frequencies of light waves are the timepieces of the universe. Waves of sunlight reaching Earth are stretched longer by 2.12 parts in a million relative to similar light waves generated on Earth. This lowering of the light wave frequency is the measure of the slowing of time. For every million Earth seconds, the Sun's clock would "lose" 2.12 seconds relative to our clocks here on Earth. The 2.12 parts per million equals 67 seconds per year, exactly the amount predicted by the laws of relativity."(52)

Taking this a step further, it's important for us to realize that the rate of time is literally different depending on where in the universe it is being measured. The rate of time measured on the sun will be different from the earth. So we need to figure from what location Genesis 1 is being narrated. Schroeder says the Hebrew language used in Genesis 1 makes it clear that time is unfolding from a God perspective, from the point of the Big Bang moving forward. So it's as if God was standing over the Big Bang and hitting a stop-watch. The correct way of examining time, according to Schroeder, is to look at the time of the universe as a whole.

The Cosmic Clock

Here is how Schroeder describes this evidence of light as a cosmic clock:

> "The lights we see in the heavens originate with energy released in stellar and galactic nuclear reactions. But there is another source of cosmic radiation, one that has been present since the creation of the universe. That is the radiation remnant, the echo as it were, of the Big Bang. This cosmic microwave background radiation (CMBR) fills the ENTIRE universe, unrelated to any particular source. Discovered by Arno Penzias and Robert Wilson in 1965, it is the only source of radiation that has been present and ubiquitous since the creation. CMBR frequency forms the basis of cosmic proper time, the biblical clock of Genesis." (55) *(emphasis added)*

Schroeder goes on to point out that this CMBR time is purely based on the stretching of space since the Big Bang and that the waves of radiation that have propagated in space since the early universe have been stretched or expanded by the same proportion that the whole universe has been expanded. This time dilation, he points out, has no relation to either the effect of gravity or velocity and so it is not based on Einstein's law of relativity. It is instead based on what is called the *redshift factor*. This *redshift factor* again confirms that the universe is a million million (one trillion) times the size it originally was and thus confirms the accuracy of cosmic proper time and its relation to local time today.

This stretching of time, according to Schroeder, gives us what scientists refer to as *cosmic time*. He says

> "The Bible's clock before Adam is not a clock tied to any one location. It is a clock that looks forward in time from the creation, encompassing the entire universe, a universal clock tuned to the cosmic radiation at the moment when matter formed. That cosmic timepiece, as observed today, ticks a million million times more slowly than at its inception. This cosmic clock records the passage of one minute while we on Earth experience a million million minutes. Genesis and science are both correct. When one asks if six days or fifteen billion years passed before the appearance of humankind, the correct answer is YES." (60)

Schroeder says this is not a far-fetched twisting of numbers but writes the following:

> "The validity of this approach, cosmic time relative to local time, has been given the stamp of approval both by the prestigious, peer-reviewed journal *Nature* (volume 342, 23: 1989) and the *American Journal of Physics* (volume 52:2; 1990)" (61).

Quark Confinement

As a double Ph.D. physicist, Schroeder now also gives a thorough explanation of the moment at the beginning of the universe at which all time began. That moment is when the energy of the Big Bang turned into MATTER. It happened, according to science, 0.00001 seconds after the Big Bang. This moment is what physicists refer to as QUARK CONFINEMENT.

According to Schroeder, we know the temperature, and hence the frequency, of radiation energy in the universe at the moment of quark confinement. He writes:

"It is not a value extrapolated or estimated from conditions in the distant past or far out in space. It is measured right here on Earth in the most advanced physics laboratories and corresponds to a temperature approximately a million-million times hotter than the current 3 degrees K temperature of the black of space. The radiation from that moment of quark confinement has been stretched a million-million fold. Its redshift, z, as observed today is 10^{12} or 1 trillion. That stretching of the light waves has slowed the frequency of the cosmic clock-expanded the perceived time between ticks of that clock-by a million million (trillion). These are solid values in physics" (59).

Using this redshift expansion number widely accepted by physicists of one trillion, Schroeder again shows that the time frame from an earth perspective might be 15.75 billion years today, but at the time that it happened, it was very close to six days. This number is achieved by dividing 15,750,000,000 (15.75 billion years) by 1,000,000,000,000 (1 trillion). This equals 0.01575 of one year. When you multiply this number by the 365 days in one year, it comes out to be a time frame of 5.75 days. Most theologians believe we are in the latter part of the sixth day.

Why Gerald Schroeder's research and books are so important is because they give strong scientific and biblical arguments for the age of the universe and they clearly show how there is no contradiction between the creation account in Genesis and the fossil record. Whenever there seems to be a contradiction between science and Scripture, it means that your depth of understanding of one or the other is flawed. It is very important that all of us be able to trust the validity of the Bible. Schroeder shows there is NO contradiction and this should give us all a great confidence in what the rest of Scripture has to say about our identity. A mature Christian has an unassailable confidence that the words of the Bible are TRUE and that they can be trusted as a FOUNDATION for life.

CHAPTER SEVEN
Mentoring to Maturity

The topic of mentorship that helps bring you to maturity could make up a whole book by itself. In this chapter, I only want to identify some key elements in the process. Although most mentoring is very organic, there also can be and probably should be some strategic intentionality to the process.

Mature people mentor others, we see from the life of Christ that He carefully and prayerfully chose his 12 key disciples. It is important to note that we are NOT called to mentor EVERYONE. We need to hear from God concerning the select few that we are to invest our time and energy into. It is also relevant to note that although Jesus selected and chose the original 12, each of them also had to choose to accept his mentorship and to follow Him.

That choice was never compulsory, and even when Jesus gave strong messages like in John 6, the Bible says "many of His disciples went back and walked with Him no more" (John 6:66). In the very next verse, Jesus says to the 12, "Do you also want to go away?" This clearly shows there was no compulsion to stay.

So in mentoring, there are two sides in dynamic tension, the initiated intentional process by a mature mentor and a voluntary participation by someone desiring to be mentored. That someone must be willing to have a reasonably high level of accountability to the one who is mentoring them.

Access
There is something extremely powerful about having access to mature people who can sow and speak into your life. This is the power of parenthood, and this is why the children of great people have such a unique advantage in their opportunity to be mentored. Unfortunately, many children of famous people become too familiar with their parents and often take for granted their input. This even happened to some degree in the family of Jesus, where His siblings had a hard time respecting or understanding His greatness because they had become too familiar with Him.

At the time that George W. Bush was President, I remember watching a wonderful live interview with his daughter, Jenna. The interviewer was asking her fascinating questions concerning her relationship with her dad and what it was like to live in the White House.

Suddenly the interviewer sprung a question on Jenna right in the heart of the interview. She asked, "Could you just call up your dad right now on the phone and talk to him?" She answered, "Sure." Seemingly from nowhere, they found a phone, with which the whole television audience could eavesdrop. She dialed an obviously secret number and guess who answered? It was the President, and it was clear he had not been expecting the call.

Jenna had to explain that she was calling from a live TV show and that their conversation was being listened to by a large audience. He was not at all upset but was so tender and loving and kind to her on that call. Most of the audience got a rare glimpse of a whole different side of the President, but what struck me was the ease of her access to her father. This is a key ingredient to mentoring. It's expected with our biological children but seldom granted to those outside of family and our intimate circles.

Jesus made access to Him the cornerstone of his discipleship and mentoring process. He had a group of 70 that were in a wider circle, then 12 that He literally lived with and finally three (Peter, James, and John) who were his inner circle. Some of Christ's deepest experiences, like His transfiguration and certain healings, were reserved for those closest three.

There is an interesting observation in the book of Acts concerning two of Jesus' closest disciples. This happened right after a crippled man had been healed at the gate of the Temple. The religious leaders were incensed that Peter and John were giving Jesus glory and proclaiming the Gospel after the healing had happened. This is how Luke describes it in the Book of Acts:

> "Now when they (the religious leaders) saw the boldness of Peter and John, and perceived that they were uneducated and untrained men, they marveled. And they realized that they had been with Jesus. And seeing how the man who had been healed standing with them, they could say nothing against it." (Acts 4:13-14 NKJV)

The leading priests realized the actions of Peter and John were directly the result of the mentorship of Jesus as there was no other explanation for their behavior nor for the power that was in their lives.

Other great Old Testament mentorship relationships in the Bible include Moses and Joshua, as well as Elijah and Elisha. In both examples, leaders successfully raised up replacements for themselves to take on the next generation. Joshua became a brilliant leader who was steadfast to the very end, and Elisha had twice as many miracles recorded through his life as Elijah. Good mentorship should bring multiplication.

Being Mentored by Reinhard Bonnke

> "It's not who you are, but who you help others become that makes the most difference."
>
> — Wellington Boone

Probably the strongest mentor in my personal life was Reinhard Bonnke. I was his employee for more than four years, but for 3 ½ of those years I lived next door to him and was part of a close-knit traveling team that went with him to the Gospel campaigns each month, normally for a period of 7-10 days at a time.

That team generally consisted of five people, Reinhard, his right-hand man Peter Vandenberg, his sound engineer Derek Murray, my wife Lisa who was the team journalist/reporter, and myself as Reinhard's TV Producer.

We traveled through airports and on planes together, and then at the crusades, we generally ate breakfast, lunch, and dinner together. I got to document Reinhard's interactions with government and national leaders, pastors, bishops and ordinary citizens. I got to see, close and personal, his reactions to criticism, how he conducted himself in front of massive crowds and around the breakfast table, his high moments and his low moments.

My favorite times were meal times. This is when I would pull out of him stories from his childhood, his dreams from the previous night or his visions for the future. A few examples of what I am sharing come readily to mind. I once asked Reinhard what was the greatest miracle healing he had ever personally witnessed in his ministry.

He immediately told of a lady who had come forward to testify with her baby in one of his crusades in Lubumbashi in Zaire. The mother was beside herself with ecstatic joy and kept on showing her baby who seemed perfectly normal. Nobody understood what had happened until she finally calmed down enough to explain that her baby had been born with male and female organs. After the prayer for the sick, she opened the baby's diaper and discovered that her child was now a perfect girl.

I especially loved hearing about the first time God used Reinhard to release a healing miracle. It happened during a prayer meeting in his father's church. Reinhard was, I think, about 11 years old and quite fearful of his father's austere rules of no moving around during a prayer meeting.

The trouble was that there was a very sick and hurting woman on the opposite side of the room who desperately needed a miracle and Reinhard suddenly got a tingling feeling in his hands together with a strong compulsion to lay hands on the lady. He tried to gently move in her direction, but his father's glare held him riveted.

Well, God's solution to elicit obedience was to turn the electricity up in Reinhard's hands. He said it felt like hundreds of volts pulsating through his fingers and it kept increasing the longer he disobeyed. He was fearful of his father but now thought the Almighty might take him out before his father could ever get to him.

The young Reinhard finally could handle it no longer and jumped up and ran towards the suffering lady. His father called out a rebuke, but Reinhard ignored it and reached the woman and laid his hands on her. She screamed as the electricity from Reinhard's hands flowed into her and instantly healed her. Now as his father came around the room to discipline Reinhard, the woman restrained him and testified that all pain had left her body the moment Reinhard had touched her. I loved these stories and loved pulling them out of Reinhard at meal times. Truth be told, I'm sure he loved sharing them.

I had access to Reinhard's video archives and to the prophecies previously given over his life. I also had the remarkable opportunity to shadow Reinhard with a camera in many parts of the world, to interview him, to interact with him, to film and document remarkable healing miracles and to journalistically verify all that happened in his ministry. It was an authentic ministry that needed no embellishment, only exposure.

There was one issue about my productions that Reinhard had trouble with. It started after I produced a documentary called *A Blood-Washed Africa* which powerfully shared Reinhard's original vision and strategy for Africa. I chose some of the most spectacular healing miracles ever captured in his work and also showed a crowd of over 5,000 in Lusaka, Zambia falling down in about five seconds under a wave of God's Holy Spirit power.

When this documentary was released, Reinhard's whole team watched it together, and everyone was deeply moved. Probably no other production that I know of helped put Reinhard's ministry on the map more than did *A Blood-Washed Africa*.

For many months Reinhard raved about this documentary and promoted it wherever he ministered in the West. Then after a trip to the USA, Reinhard approached me and said, "Berin, I no longer like this *A Blood-Washed Africa* movie." I was astonished, how was it possible his tastes had suddenly changed after this program had done so much good to promote his ministry?

Reinhard's explanation made me laugh. He said that wherever he went to minister, this video had been sent ahead to promote his visit. The documentary literally showed some of the greatest highlights of his work, but not his normal everyday life. "The problem," Reinhard said "is that when I come to a church, the people think the Apostle Paul has arrived." Reinhard felt the movie created an unrealistic expectation of his ministry and that was why he no longer liked that amazing documentary.

The truth is that Reinhard did have an extraordinary ministry and something supernatural could happen at any time during one of his meetings. When I was on the crusade platform with him, I would use one eye to film the massive crowds, miracles, and healings, and the other eye to watch the dynamics of these events. I always desired to discern and discover the spiritual and natural elements that enabled God to use Reinhard to save and heal so many people.

Although Reinhard had not defined it, he had granted me access and close exposure to himself and to his mature ministry and life. He was mentoring me and became an incredible spiritual father to me. No other season of growth in my life had a more formative impact on me than the years I spent with Reinhard. Even now, more than 25 years later, I will daily quote phrases and anecdotes that I picked up from him. You will notice them peppered throughout this book.

Paul Mentoring Timothy
The most critical elements in mentoring are access, time interacting, personal example, and a desire to teach and impart all that you know to others. It is true spiritual parenting. A huge New Testament example is Paul's relationship with Timothy. Paul called him a spiritual son and wrote these words to him:

> "But you have carefully followed my doctrine, manner of life, purpose, faith, longsuffering, love, perseverance, persecutions, afflictions, which happened to me at Antioch, at Iconium, at Lystra—what persecutions I endured. And out of them all the LORD delivered me."
> (2 Timothy 3:10-11 NKJV)

Paul allowed Timothy to have full access to every part of his life, including his trials and afflictions. Most importantly he taught Timothy his doctrine, manner of life, his purpose and his faith. It was the three mentoring pillars of access, example and teaching that are revealed in what we know of this relationship.

Paul held nothing back and allowed Timothy to see his trials and tribulations. He let Timothy travel with him so he could experience ministry first hand. His two letters to Timothy are full of mentoring wisdom and instruction. The fact that Paul wrote such letters to Timothy reveals a huge amount about the close nature of their relationship.

A few years ago a friend of mine, Tony Cooke wrote a wonderful book titled *In Search of Timothy*. Tony is a remarkable Bible teacher and was originally the head of Kenneth Hagin's Rhema Bible College program in Tulsa, Oklahoma. His book tells of the need for true assistants like Timothy to come alongside God's present-day leaders in Christian ministry. When Tony came to our church a few years back, I complimented him on his book but challenged him to write a sequel. He looked at me with a puzzled expression, "What sequel?" he asked. I said to him, "You need to write a book titled *In Search of Paul* because unless the Christian world raises up more Pauls, we cannot expect to find Timothys.

Mentoring Young People and Modern-Day Timothys

When it comes to interactions with teenagers and youth, I caution people to follow some strict guidelines, especially with all the abuse that has happened to kids in our generation. It is wisdom to err on the side of openness and accountability. When I communicate with young people, I am very transparent with their parents and expect that anything and everything I text, write, email or share with them can, should and likely will be shared with their parents. I actually don't mind if a kid is in another state or even another country. It reduces things down to heart-to-heart communication and removes even the notion of inappropriate physical interaction.

Personal interaction with kids and teens must ALWAYS be guided by what is **appropriate**. Things, like going to a sports game or playing a sports game with a young person, is often a great way to connect with them. Going to church with them is also something positive to do with them and their family, and I often will invite them to volunteer a few hours of service in our office where they can be productive and be around a lot of other godly young people. Very often parents are comfortable allowing you to have a meal in a public area with a teen, again, accountability, trust and transparency are key factors. Of course, if you are ever able to employ them in some capacity to work alongside of you and learn skills, and especially in Kingdom endeavors, that is always a great way to mentor. Finally, I should give a shout out for camps and missions trips. These provide quality time with young people in an accountable space. My wife and I have literally taken hundreds of individuals and families all over the world on missions trips and truly been able to build amazing relationships through those endeavors.

Sometimes navigating these kinds of relationships takes the wisdom of Solomon, but I always act as if everything I write or say or do is going to be written in the newspapers of tomorrow. I treat other people's kids as if they were my own children and always think of what will be in their best interests. I also draw on more than 40 years of experience in mentoring young people, going back to my days as a prefect (person in charge) at that Hilton College boarding school in South Africa through to running a preschool in Nigeria, and being a children's pastor in charge of 1,200 kids in California.

Although I don't currently hold those responsibilities, I generally, at any one time, am taking a reasonable time to mentor at least five or six young people in their faith and in their walk with God. I find myself teaching them the principles of friendship and relationship that people like Reinhard Bonnke taught me. I find that my example and my genuine care for them is a critical part of the equation and again, how things might be perceived is always guiding me. I think frequently and intentionally about how others might view my interactions.

Of course, as young people turn 18 and mature into adulthood, the nature of the communication with them will often change, and more adult topics can be broached. They often just need to know that your ear is always open to hearing their needs and that you will pray for them and with them when they face difficult decisions or crises.

Many of those I mentored years ago are now in their thirties with families of their own. I'm thrilled whenever I see them take others under their wing and begin mentoring them. Some have had me do things like officiate their weddings or attend their graduations and most stay in regular communication with me. Just because society today has created so many minefields, does not mean that we should avoid close friendships and communication with others. We need to pray daily that God delivers us from evil, but we also need to be guided by two things: 1) make sure that everything you do is appropriate, and 2) make sure you are aware of how everything you do, say and write will be perceived.

The truth is we desperately need more spiritual fathers and mothers in the Christian world. We not only need good Christian parents to help raise our natural children but we also need outside mentors to help bring young believers to maturity.

CHAPTER EIGHT

Employment as a Vehicle of Mentoring

"If you really want to get to know the true character of someone, let them become your boss."

— Author unknown

I mentioned that what enabled my mentorship by Reinhard Bonnke was being employed as his television producer. I am not advocating employment as the only means of mentorship, but I am saying it's a very good vehicle. I have often said that if I had an extra million dollars, I would hire an additional 100 people and mentor them. I currently employ more than 50 people between my ministry and the two preschools my wife and I manage. Many of them are young people, and most of the key people in my ministry are those I have mentored in the workplace for a significant number of years. I truly believe that the greatest test of a person's ministry and leadership is not how strong their ministry gift is, but is found in their ability to build and finance a team. Employing others will test every character quality, skill and sense of faith a leader thinks they have.

What are the advantages of employment when it comes to mentorship? I recently shared on this topic and broke the process down into eight aspects that all begin with the letter *D*. These eight things are what make employment such a powerful mentoring vehicle:

1. You can put a **Demand** on people's gifts, talent and calling and help to develop them. Many years ago I discovered an awkward young homeschooled kid by the name of Paul Black. He would bring a VHS camera to children's church and was passionate about media. At the age of 12, I took him into my office as a volunteer to help take out the trash and do menial tasks. By 15 he had his own editing bay in my media department, and I began training him in television production. Soon after he turned 20, I created a youth television series called *YouthBytes* and teamed Paul with Chad Daniel, a powerful youth minister, and media expert coming out of Joyce Meyer Ministries. I put a demand on the gifts in Paul and Chad and forced them each year to grow and develop their skills.

YouthBytes today airs weekly, not only on the Daystar Network but on over 800 television stations around the world in numerous languages. Chad's personal ministry has literally become a juggernaut in its own right, especially in the nation of Brazil where thousands of young people flock to his youth rallies. *YouthBytes* has now produced more than 60 dynamic high energy episodes and has 30 half-hour television broadcast shows shot in over 15 countries. It all happened because I was able to put a demand on the gifts, talents, and callings in these two amazing people and the team that works around them.

2. You can **Develop** a person's abilities and character. Jesus said to Peter and Andrew:

"Follow Me, and I will make you fishers of men" (Matthew 4:19 NKJV).

Jesus was literally saying, "Follow me and I will help mentor you so that you become evangelists." He saw the untapped potential and callings in their lives and was volunteering to draw out and develop those gifts in them. Good mentors discern the five-fold graces in others and volunteer to mentor those graces to maturity.

3. You can **Disciple** a person in their faith. Being employed by Reinhard did more to disciple me in my faith than ten years in seminary would have done. Being on the front lines of world evangelism in front of crowds numbering in the hundreds of thousands forced my faith to grow and stretch and develop. I literally saw God's Word come alive as millions responded to salvation and I watched as prayer brought about miracles and healings in people's lives. Many times I was faced with huge technical challenges during the crusades, and many times I saw God perform miracles to help my co-workers and me.

One time we were in front of a crowd of 150,000 in Lagos, Nigeria. My good friend, Derek Murray, was Reinhard's sound engineer and we often were thrown into the deep end together on projects and in crisis situations. This particular meeting Reinhard had just explained to the huge crowd the baptism with the Holy Spirit and had come to the critical moment in the meeting where he was about to pray for that gift to be given to them. Suddenly Derek's entire soundboard just quit working, and Reinhard literally had no sound going through the amplifiers. Derek was in the deep end swimming, and I had no clue how to help him. What I did have was a small half-inch to mini jack connector for my video equipment.

On the spur of the moment, God gave Derek an ingenious solution. While those on the platform floundered, Derek sent a young man to retrieve this tiny audio adapter from me on the opposite side of the platform. He used a small professional Sony cassette player to give him a line in/line out preamp signal and ran a single microphone directly through the cassette player into the amplifiers. Miraculously we now had a signal and Reinhard, and his interpreter was able to finish the meeting on one shared microphone. Reinhard prayed for the Holy Spirit, and tens of thousands received that wonderful gift. Derek's faith and mine both grew significantly that day.

I try and keep that same discipleship going in my own staff today as we step on the waters of faith for tens of thousands of dollars each week to sustain our current ministry work. In 26 years we have never missed a payroll and God has always been faithful, but not without us having to fight and work and stretch our faith daily, and weekly, and monthly. Employment is such a powerful vehicle to disciple people in the realities of using their faith and finding creative solutions.

4. You can **Deposit** vision and values into a person. I remember being at Reinhard's conference table at his headquarters in Frankfurt, Germany. Reinhard hit the table with his large and powerful hand. "I have a vision," Reinhard said with his distinctive German accent, "God wants us to do a conference to reach the whole of Europe." Reinhard never dreamed small. We already were engaged monthly in doing huge campaigns in Africa, but now Reinhard was speaking about a Eurofire conference to massively impact Europe.

Our small team looked at each other and saw only four letters: W-O-R-K. Reinhard instilled vision in us, and we carried his values and carried out that vision as well as his values. We ended up pulling together a conference in July of 1988 in Birmingham, England where 20,000 people came from all over Europe. The event was brilliantly planned and executed by Rob Birkbeck, who now coordinates the global distribution of John Bevere's materials. We had the Eurofire meetings translated live into 11 European languages. There were 17 live seminar venues where audio recordings were simultaneously happening, and there were four live multi-camera television venues also operating at the same time. My budget for the technical side of that event was at least a half a million dollars. Eurofire ended up being a spectacular watershed event for the whole continent of Europe, and we sold over $150,000 worth of video and audiocassette material during the four-day conference in all 11 languages.

Reinhard certainly was the greatest visionary I have ever worked for, and his vision was infectious. Through that single event in 1988, the groundwork was also laid technically for the subsequent development of the multilingual recordings of the ISOM, which used a similar technique to what we had pioneered in Europe.

5. You can require personal **Discipline** in a person's work ethic and behavior. I have a whole chapter following on the topic of discipline but simply need to say here that employment provides a structured workday that is such a help to instill discipline

in people's lives. Currently, my ministry produces a weekly 15-minute television production that involves a discussion between my assistant Brad Andrews and I. This is made for the hundreds of ISOM online students that study weekly from home and through mobile devices. It also becomes part of a growing online archive for future ISOM students to access and view.

Paul Black has turned the office adjacent to mine into a mini TV studio with a very pleasing compact set that we use for this purpose. We call the production *ISOM Connect* and each week Brad and I get more and more adept at interacting with each other and the broader ISOM audience. We have also begun doing Facebook Live® seminars, and we have a strict schedule of posting things out onto social media.

Our overall office continues daily to process orders, diplomas, and degrees from around the world and, most of the time functions like a well-oiled machine. I have at least five different reports generated each day informing me on the health of each area of the ministry so I can keep my finger on the pulse of things no matter where I am in the world. All this requires us to enforce disciplined operational functions in the lives of every employee, and that disciplined functionality enables us to keep achieving great things for God.

6. You can instill **Dignity** and self-respect in people's lives. I love this quote:

> "Never take a person's dignity:
> it is worth everything to them, and nothing to you."
>
> — Frank Barron

Before most people believe in themselves, they often need others they respect to believe in them. When I began producing YouthBytes, it seems like the whole world was against me. The cry of my heart was to reach the upcoming teenage generation with a powerful media based tool. I knew that if we as the global Church failed to reach the youth, that there would be no pastors coming up through the ranks and no missionaries being sent out in the future to reach the lost.

The production costs each month for YouthBytes was over $30,000 and the opposition was very strong. It first came from my board of directors who grumbled about its costs and perceived effectiveness. Then my own staff complained that there was no budget for other things because of *YouthBytes*. Then my closest advisors piled on saying they felt I was not running in my right lane. Finally, Chad came to me and began voicing his doubts. I stopped him in his tracks. I said: "Chad if God wants to take down the entire ministry, I'm willing to go down with it. I'm not quitting *YouthBytes*."

Chad was stunned because nobody had ever believed in him like that before and nobody had ever stood with him like that. He picked himself up and, together with Paul Black, made *YouthBytes* an international success. Sometimes people just need you to believe in them, invest in them, stand with them and respect their dignity and calling.

7. You can help **Direct** people in the way they need to go in their career. Reinhard always used to say, "Some people are called to a ministry, and some people are called through a ministry." When I was with him, I knew that God was using him to mentor my life but that my ultimate calling lay on the other side of the harvest. I knew I was not called to crusade evangelism, but to help develop and support pastors and leaders in the job of discipling those won to Christ to maturity.

Before Lisa and I left Reinhard, we did two ten-day fasts. I knew God was calling us on, but I loved Reinhard and wanted the transition to be done right. God showed me the exact day to tell Reinhard, and God prepared his heart for the transition. Afterward, he said to me, "Berin, the way you have done this has been exemplary." I could not have had a higher compliment.

I view every employee in Good Shepherd Ministries as a sacred stewardship. Jesus owns every one of them, and I get to steward each life for whatever season God gives them to us. My ultimate goal is to prepare them the best that I can for their future callings, and I work to mentor and develop their faith and their characters, so they succeed in the long term in whatever career God calls them to. Some are lifers in Good Shepherd, and others are being readied for greater things outside my ministry. I need to rejoice whenever God allows me to have any part in the development of others.

8. You can **Demonstrate** the love and character of God in servanthood to your employees. We know that one of the last acts of Jesus was to wash the feet of His disciples. This was so humbling to Peter that he tried refusing to allow Jesus to do this. Jesus said to Peter: *"If I do not wash you, you have no part with Me"* (John 13:8 NKJV).

It's critical for our staff at Good Shepherd to know that Lisa and I are there ultimately to serve them. We are often willing to sacrifice our own salaries to keep them employed. We sometimes are the last to take benefits because we are called to serve and love and bless others before ourselves. We are willing to work the late hours and weekends, solving problems, answering emails and fixing mistakes. We believe this is simply the least we need to be doing for our staff and team. Lisa and I both learned this from Reinhard. Lisa would work back and forth with Reinhard, editing his articles and Revival Report Magazine late at night even up until midnight. Reinhard himself worked and prayed and gave of himself more than us all, but he also taught us and mentored into us that servanthood mentality and ethics.

Creating a Right Environment for Mentorship
In our ministry the first half hour of every day is prayer, and everyone is on the clock. My staff is literally being paid to pray. This helps foster a godly atmosphere in our office, and it helps to set the right priorities and build team unity.

As you walk into the upstairs area of our office where the team prays daily, we have a framed statement on the wall outlining the type of environment we strive for in our office. The idea came years ago with the statement of a lady who was visiting us in California. She simply said, "When God created the world, He spent six days creating an environment, and then He put man into that environment."

That's all I needed to hear. I suddenly understood how important a good environment is and have striven ever since to create good environments in my home, in my office, in our preschools and in any event our ministry does. So on the wall, we set a goal for the following distinctives in our office environment. We always want to strive to create:

- An environment of grace and forgiveness.
- An environment of truthfulness, integrity, and honesty.
- An environment that fosters growth and learning.
- An environment that promotes justice and fairness.
- An environment where every person's dignity is respected.
- An environment of protection and security.
- An environment of creativity and an environment where thinking out of the box is encouraged.
- An environment that encourages fun, enjoyment and the celebration of life.
- An environment free of hypocrisy and compromise.
- An environment that fosters open communication.
- An environment of accountability.
- An environment of affirmation and encouragement.
- An environment where people feel genuinely loved and cared for.

We also highlight some of the elements that can quickly poison an environment:

- Envy and self-seeking — James 3:16
- Wrong motivations
- Greed, Strife, Gossip, Hypocrisy, Pride
- Control, manipulation and the misuse of power
- Fear and insecurity – people not knowing where they stand
- Mistrust, deception, and deceit – not having vulnerability and transparency in our dealings
- Partiality, injustice, and unfairness or an unjust scale
- Unrighteousness, Oppression, Intimidation, Prejudice

So through these goals and warnings, we work very hard to create an environment in which every team member can flourish and grow. After prayer in our office is over every morning, we roll up our sleeves and work extremely hard to make ends meet. I try and pay every employee in a way that honors their skill, gifting, and productivity. I believe that if you want to demand accountability from an employee, then you need to take a lot of responsibility for their lives and needs.

Employment Mentorship in Scripture
A very inspirational parable that Jesus told in Matthew 20:1-16 NLT has strongly impacted my perspective on employment. In this parable, Jesus likens the Kingdom of Heaven to a landowner who goes out at the beginning of a day to hire laborers for his vineyard.

> "For the Kingdom of Heaven is like the landowner who went out early one morning to hire workers for his vineyard. He agreed to pay the normal daily wage and sent them out to work.
>
> At nine o'clock in the morning he was passing through the marketplace and saw some people standing around doing nothing. So he hired them, telling them he would pay them whatever was right at the end of the day. So they went to work in the vineyard.
>
> At noon and again at three o'clock he did the same thing. At five o'clock that afternoon he was in town again and saw some more people standing around. He asked them, "Why haven't you been working today?" They replied, "Because no one hired us." The landowner told them, "Then go out and join the others in my vineyard."

That evening he told the foreman to call the workers in and pay them, beginning with the last workers first. When those hired at five o'clock were paid, each received a full day's wage. When those hired first came to get their pay, they assumed they would receive more. But they, too, were paid a day's wage.

When they received their pay, they protested to the owner, "Those people worked only one hour, and yet you've paid them just as much as you paid us who worked all day in the scorching heat."

"He answered one of them, "Friend, I haven't been unfair! Didn't you agree to work all day for the usual wage? Take your money and go. I wanted to pay this last worker the same as you. Is it against the law for me to do what I want with my money? Should you be jealous because I am kind to others?" So those who are last now will be first then, and those who are first will be last.

There are some fascinating insights in this parable concerning God's heart towards employment. Jesus, through this parable, makes it clear that God absolutely wants everyone employed and especially in His Kingdom. I believe this desire of God also extends into the natural workplace.

Employing every possible person is such a passion for the landowner that he goes looking multiple times during the same day for employees to hire. He clearly has a problem with people being idle and says to those he finds, "Why haven't you been working today?" God wants people gainfully employed in both the natural world and in building His Kingdom.

The second amazing point in this parable is that the landowner pays everyone the same amount. This is counterintuitive and goes against all the norms of sound practice that most businesses run by. Only looking deeper at the heart of the landowner and his perspective on employment does this landowner's practice even vaguely make sense.

It's clear from this parable that the landowner was hiring, not so much for his own benefit, but for the benefit of the employees. He is almost looking for an excuse to pay the employees and provide resources to them. He obviously wants to give them dignity in legitimately earning wages, but his employment is less about the productivity he can get out of them and more about what he can deposit into them.

The landowner's only criteria for a full daily pay provision in this parable was a commitment by each laborer to "join the others in my vineyard." Once you commit yourself to join God's labor force, He will commit to a full provision of your needs. How should this impact employment in the secular world? In a normal workplace, the heart of an employer needs to see employees as joining a family where every member gets to feel like they can partake in the provision of the family.

The expectation of the employees in Christ's parable is that they will be compensated based on how LONG they had worked on that specific day. Jesus turns that thinking on its head when the landowner says: "I wanted to pay this last worker the same as you. Is it against the law for me to do what I want with my money? Should you be jealous because I am kind to others?" (Matthew 20:5).

The focus here is on the heart, desire, and goodwill of the EMPLOYER regardless of who the employee is or how LONG they had worked. So employment in God's eyes is a way to bless and help people so long as they wholeheartedly commit to join and work for a family, a cause and a team. In the natural, it's a beautiful doorway into the process of developing and mentoring a person's life.

Another wonderful Old Testament example of this principle at work is in the story of Ruth and Boaz. Here is how the book of Ruth describes the employment relationship between Ruth and Boaz:

> Then Boaz asked his foreman, "Who is that young woman over there? Who does she belong to?" And the foreman replied, "She is the young woman from Moab who came back with Naomi. She asked me this morning if she could gather grain behind the harvesters. She has been hard at work ever since, except for a few minutes rest in the shelter."
>
> Boaz went over and said to Ruth, "Listen, my daughter. Stay right here with us when you gather grain; don't go to any other fields. Stay right behind the young women working in my field. See which part of the field they are harvesting, and then follow them. I have warned the young men not to treat you roughly. And when you are thirsty, help yourself to the water they have drawn from the well. Ruth fell at his feet and thanked him warmly. "What have I done to deserve such kindness?" she asked. "I am only a foreigner." "Yes, I know," Boaz replied. "But I also know about everything you have done for your mother-in-law since the death of your husband. I have heard how you

left your father and mother and your own land to live here among complete strangers. May the LORD, the God of Israel, under whose wings you have come to take refuge, reward you fully for what you have done" (Ruth 2:5–12 NLT).

When Ruth went back to work again, Boaz ordered his young men, "Let her gather grain right among the sheaves without stopping her. And pull out some heads of barley from the bundles and drop them on purpose for her. Let her pick them up, and don't give her a hard time!" So Ruth gathered barley there all day, and when she beat out the grain that evening, it filled an entire basket.

Then Ruth said, "What's more, Boaz even told me to come back and stay with his harvesters until the entire harvest is completed."

So Ruth worked alongside the women in Boaz's fields and gathered grain with them until the end of the barley harvest. Then she continued working with them through the wheat harvest in early summer. And all the while she lived with her mother-in-law."
(Ruth 2:15–17, 21, 23 NLT).

Here are some amazing parallel insights from a real-life employer and his employees. We must understand that Ruth was a foreigner from the tribe of Moab, a people group normally despised in Israel. She was also trying desperately to get food for her mother-in-law Naomi and herself. She decided to glean whatever scraps she could get behind the harvesters in the field of Boaz.

From this whole account, we can see that the foreman and laborers of Boaz treated him with great respect. The foreman communicated with him accurately what was taking place in the workplace, including the addition of Ruth as a gleaner. From all that we know and can tell, the laborers also fully obeyed every directive and instruction Boaz gave them throughout the story.

Boaz somehow knew of the loyalty of Ruth to Naomi so his first kindnesses to her may have been due to an appreciation and respect for the way Ruth had treated his relative. He definitely did not know who she was at the beginning of this narrative because he asked his foreman, "Who is that young woman over there?" Whatever his motivation, Boaz used his influence as the 'boss' to protect Ruth physically, telling her, "I have warned the young men not to treat you roughly," and in another place, he told his young men. "Don't give her a hard time!"

CHAPTER 8: EMPLOYMENT AS A VEHICLE OF MENTORING

Boaz was also interested in putting Ruth with good people and made sure she had good influences around her. He knew in other fields she might be taken advantage of so he made sure Ruth stayed under his employment covering and with those he had trained and trusted. Here is how the Scriptures describe the words of Boaz to Ruth: "Stay right here with us when you gather grain; don't go to any other fields. Stay right behind the young women working in my field. See which part of the field they are harvesting, and then follow them." It's not a stretch to say that Boaz wanted Ruth mentored.

The concern Boaz showed for Ruth was not momentary. The Bible says, "So Ruth worked alongside the women in Boaz's fields and gathered grain with them until the end of the barley harvest. Then she continued working with them through the wheat harvest in early summer." Boaz made sure when one project was over (the barley harvest), that another one opened up (the wheat harvest). Employers MUST work to provide ongoing employment to their employees because they are not just disposable commodities.

Boaz then went out of his way to make sure Ruth's need for food and provision were met. The Scriptures describe it like this: Boaz ordered his young men, "Let her gather grain right among the sheaves without stopping her. And pull out some heads of barley from the bundles and drop them on purpose for her."

It seems like on the first day Ruth met Boaz, he was practicing the 'gleaning' principle with Ruth. He made sure enough barley was left behind for Ruth as this narrative indicates: "So Ruth gathered barley there all day, and when she beat out the grain that evening, it filled an entire basket." It seems like she did NOT do this for long because she went home and told Naomi, "Boaz even told me to come back and stay with his harvesters until the entire harvest is completed." It appears obvious from the story that she gleaned for a while and then got hired.

With such love and care, it's no wonder that Ruth fell in love with Boaz. Boaz did not seem to realize until the end of this story that Ruth might become his future wife. Because she was a foreigner, marriage with a Jew would have been frowned upon, but there was a Jewish legal precedent stronger than her nationality. Ruth had been married to a Jewish man, and the Torah required that when a husband died, that a brother or close relative needed to marry the widow and raise up children for the family.

When Boaz suddenly understood the possibility that he could become a kinsman redeemer, he first needed to check whether a closer relative would take her. When that did not work out, he married this special, amazing employee whom he had treated with dignity, protection, and respect from the first day she had arrived on the job. What a marvelous love story but also what a wonderful example of a wise and godly employer.

From the way Boaz treated a lowly employee, he ended up getting a loyal and godly wife. She became the great grandmother of King David, and she became a part of the royal lineage of Jesus.

The Dangers of Success
I want to close out this chapter by looking at the dangers of success. Years ago we recorded an incredible two-part video series on the topic of betrayal. I flew our cameras and crew all the way to the Philippines to get this phenomenal series from David Sumrall, pastor at that time of a 35,000-member church in the city of Manila. I share more on how we got this series in the chapter coming up on "Maturity and Truth."

David had been through many betrayals and had finally cried out to God for wisdom in this difficult area. The Lord answered by opening up a profound understanding concerning the betrayal by Judas of Jesus. David's teachings in this series have helped so many people, but I only want to point out one specific point David made in the series that's relative to the point of this chapter. David said that every betrayal he had personally experienced was the result of relating to people the way they USED TO BE, and NOT the way they CURRENTLY ARE. His point was that PEOPLE CHANGE. That change may be subtle and slow but, over time, it can easily happen.

I heard once about an ancient conversation from about the 5th Century AD that was recorded in ancient literature between a Bishop and a Cardinal. For roughly the first four centuries of Christianity, believers were horribly persecuted, beaten, imprisoned, tortured, and thrown to lions and wild animals to be torn apart. Then Constantine converted and everything changed. It suddenly became dangerous to NOT be a Christian. The result was that the Church gained political power, wealth, beautiful buildings and overall prosperity.

This conversation between the Bishop and the Cardinal purportedly happened after this transition to wealth had taken place. At the time of the conversation, both church leaders were gorgeously arrayed in beautiful garments. They were inside a magnificent cathedral with gold and silver goblets, communion serving plates and gold candelabra all around. Supposedly the Cardinal looked around at his royal environment and remarked to the Bishop, "I guess we can no longer say like the Apostle Peter did in the book of Acts that 'silver and gold have I none.'" To which the Bishop responded, "That's true, but the tragedy is that neither can we say, like Peter did to the crippled man in the Book of Acts, in the Name of Jesus rise up and walk."

The Church had gained the wealth, protection and prosperity of the Roman Empire but had lost the power of God. This danger of the 'deceitfulness of riches' still exists today and is especially threatening when churches gain a margin of success. As my best friend and founding pastor of The Rock Church and World Outreach Center, Jim Cobrae, once remarked, "There are a 100 people who can survive and deal with failure, but only one in a 100 who can handle success."

Almost every person who pioneers a church does it for the right reasons. People put their whole lives on the line as they sacrifice financial security in order to build a new work for God. The difficult process requires long hours of prayer, relentless evangelism, lonely moments of discouragement without support, and frequent persecution. These challenges normally keep a pioneer pastor spiritually close to God.

Churches and leaders have to be careful that as their congregations grow, they don't move from:

- Being people oriented to becoming task oriented.
- Being God promoting to becoming self-promoting.
- Trusting in anointing to trusting in image.
- Being a family of God to becoming an organization of man.
- Focusing on prayer, patience, and perseverance to focusing on procedure, process, and politics.
- Honoring relationship and faithfulness to honoring only professionalism and productivity.
- Meeting the needs of people to being driven by money, management, and appearance.
- Focusing on calling, character, and commitment to focusing on credentials, charisma, and contracts.
- Being a place where the gifts of people are identified, developed and released to a place where gifts are coveted, contained and concealed.

Each of these could be covered in a chapter, and each may seem like far fetched transitions, but I got this list by watching and observing many of these changes actually happen in real churches and ministries that I know. An honest reading of the books of first and second Kings, and first and second Chronicles in the Old Testament shows one startling fact, that is that very few of the kings and rulers of Israel and Judah finished well. Many started well, but most got derailed somewhere along the way.

This is why there are certain things every Christian must do to help keep them on track and to help them keep progressing towards maturity. For myself, it's daily disciplined times of prayer and taking groups of people to the mission fields of the world each year. These things help keep my perspective grounded and my priorities right. As I previously mentioned in Chapter 4, my best friend Jim Cobrae and his wife Deborah, built **The Rock Church and World Outreach Center**, a 10,000-member church in San Bernardino, California. The Rock, without any strings attached, feeds about 500,000 people all their groceries throughout the year.

A few times a week, lines of people with baskets stretch for long distances outside the food distribution area at the rear side of The Rock. Very often in those lines, you will see a tall guy with a baseball cap handing out groceries. Most of the time nobody in the line recognizes him, but that's the founding pastor, Jim Cobrae, just keeping his heart on track with God.

Handing out groceries keeps Jim grounded, and seeing those needy families helps him maintain a right perspective of why he started pastoring. One time he complained to God that even though they were feeding so many people, almost none of them were coming to his church. He felt God answer back, "Because you feed them, I come to your church." All we really need is for God to show up and speak to His people when they gather together.

So what about you, what are the things that you need to do to keep your life on track? Let's explore this a little deeper as we look at the terrible but wonderful "*D*" word DISCIPLINE.

CHAPTER NINE

Maturity and Discipline

"Discipline is just choosing between what you want now and what you want most."

— Unknown

This chapter is one of the most difficult for me to write because, in so many ways, I don't yet feel I have conquered this mountain. There are a number of areas where I believe God has given me some great insight when it comes to discipline, but others where I see friends and colleagues far ahead of me. I actually finished writing all the other chapters of this book and then came back to tackle this one.

Diego Mesa – Overcoming Stage IV Kidney Cancer

"You have to be tougher than your toughest day."

— Diego Mesa

There are probably three specific people who have challenged my walk with God in this area of discipline. The first is Diego Mesa, pastor of a 16,000-member church in Rancho Cucamonga, California. Diego is also a survivor of Stage IV kidney cancer. His doctors told him that he probably had a year to live and that in the medical history of cases with his diagnosis, nobody had ever lived longer than six years. As I write this, Diego has just crossed the 10-year survival mark. He and I regularly play golf together and, to my shame, he regularly beats me.

Diego did not have one of those instantaneous miracle healing stories. His was a sheer battle of grit, determination, faith, and discipline. I will let him describe a little of this battle in his own words as written in his book ***How to Dream When You're Told You're Going to Die***:

> "Many Christians, when facing a mountain or challenge, don't dig deep or do anything more than they have been previously doing. They don't show a serious commitment to fight.
>
> I believe that in the spiritual battles we fight, sometimes we need to get just plain ornery as we take our stand against the enemy. When I was sick, I remember times when I simply felt terrible and didn't

want to do anything. But I would tell myself, the devil isn't taking a day off. Why should I? Get up, Diego! Whether you like it or not, and whether you want to or not, do something.

You have to be tougher than your toughest day. If the devil is going to use everything he can to defeat us, why not use everything at our disposal to fight against him and persevere? If he is going to throw the kitchen sink at you, throw it back. If he is not going to give up or back down, neither do you!

Some people are born fighters. Others are much more passive by nature and have to learn to take a stand when its called for. Even the meekest people will push back when the situation calls for it. It may be a mother protecting a child, a senior citizen being neglected in a retirement home, a student fed up with being bullied, or any number of other injustices. Press the right buttons, and almost anyone will gear up for a fight. All of us have the ability, but we need to direct our passion toward overcoming our adversity and defeating our spiritual enemy. Get ornery, mean and bothered toward the devil and fight with all your might (59, 60).

What does "being ornery" look like? It meant I was going to fight the attack with my thoughts, words, actions, attitude, spiritual disciplines, medicines, nutrition, exercise and everything else I could think of" (61).

Diego began confessing 175 healing Scriptures over his life every single day. He had these on a tattered piece of paper in his Bible. That paper was covered in tears as he wept and confessed those words to God. He then changed everything in his life. His rest patterns, his food intake, his exercise routine, his thoughts, his words, his spiritual disciplines, his water intake, his associations and what he allowed his eyes to see and take in. Diego studied food and proper nutrition. He spent three days with Jordan Rubin, learning how to eat better.

To this day, Diego is one of the most disciplined people I know. It took more than two years for Diego to really start feeling the victory coming. During that time he faithfully took the medication prescribed to him. However, when he sensed in himself the healing begin to grip and when his faith and disciplined life began to dominate his disease, at that point he threw the Sutent chemotherapy pills he had been taking into the Atlantic Ocean, and he has not looked back.

Diego still follows a daily discipline of God's Word, of right eating, exercise, rest and water intake that does not deviate from what God showed him during that epic battle for his life. Recently I asked Diego about another pastor who was suffering from a major kidney problem and questioned him why some things might not be working as effectively for that man as they were for Diego. Diego's answer still cuts me to the heart. He said, when it comes to the discipline in his life, he does not cheat.

Diego won that battle for his own testimony. He won it for his church, for his family, for his children and grandchildren, for every person out there who is suffering from cancer or for any diagnosis where the doctors have all but given up. He won it for the world because we now have recorded that testimony, and are getting it out all over the world in multiple languages. He has put his battle into the book quoted previously, and Diego is now on television weekly sharing about the power and goodness of God. The devil will pay dearly for that attack against Diego's health because that testimony will defeat him everywhere.

Dave Hodgson – From Soldier to Kingdom Minded Entrepreneur

> "The man who can drive himself further once the effort gets painful is the man who will win."
>
> — Roger Bannister
> (the first person to run a mile in less than four minutes)

The second person who has challenged me in the area of discipline has been Dave Hodgson. Dave is now in his sixties and lives in Australia. He was originally a soldier, being in special ops both as a Selous Scout and a soldier with the Special Air Service (SAS). The Selous Scouts were the Green Berets of the Rhodesian (now Zimbabwe) army, and the SAS is a special-forces unit of the British army. These are some of the most dangerous people in a theatre of war. They are so well trained that they often know their enemy better than their enemy knows themselves. They are the elite of the elite when it comes to the disciplined execution of a plan.

Dave has brought that kind of discipline and strategic thought into the building of God's Kingdom. The areas God has assigned him to take territory is that of business, education, politics, and whatever other areas of the marketplace he can influence. He has both a short-term and a long-term strategy. His immediate goal is to turn Australia into the world's first "Sheep Nation" as described by Christ in Matthew 25.

Dave has divided the world up into time regions. His normal day starts at 4 AM and ends at midnight. One day a week is set aside to pray and seek God. The other days revolve around the workdays in different parts of the world. So when America is open for business, Dave books Skype® calls and interactions with that region during those hours. As the world turns and Europe and Africa get up for business, Dave shifts his focus to that region of the world. Finally, as the world turns some more, Dave sets up his business calls into Asia and Australia. The result is that Dave is able to manage a group of more than 30 companies spanning the globe. Those companies now are worth more than a billion dollars.

Dave is just getting started. The real purpose of wealth for him is the influence it provides him into the marketplace. He continually is using his financial platform to speak into the secular realm words designed to change the culture of business. He does not speak Christianese, rather he speaks to business leaders about a *preferred economy* that is not based on greed and corruption but instead based on *sharing, caring and universal prosperity*. He promotes a business philosophy where everyone benefits in transactions and where every deal done is a win for all parties.

Dave takes every interview with the media that he possibly can handle, and most weekends he travels the world speaking to business people in churches about their role in taking territory for God in the marketplace. In Chapter 13 I share more on how Dave navigates church speaking engagements and focus there on how Dave handles honorariums. Dave has a tremendous study discipline, and he tirelessly researches the history of famous Scripture passages to pull out the deep marketplace relevance of what took place in many popular Old and New Testament stories. Stories like that of Moses and his role in Egypt's military or of Matthew and Zacchaeus and the relationship of Jesus to the tax collectors of his day. Dave's discipline and research often provide some stunning marketplace insights that are very relevant to the present.

All of this requires Dave to stay in excellent health and physical condition. Dave is also now growing more and more savvy at using Internet technology to deliver his messages to ever-increasing audiences. His primary message to those in the Marketplace is for them NEVER to allow the spirit of Mammon to have ANY place in their heart or their affairs. That Babylonian culture and spirit will cut off God's ability to work in a person's life and business and only with it GONE can you truly prosper in a Kingdom culture. Staying in that culture requires doing things God's way, both in a person's personal lifestyle and in every business decision. Dave stays very accountable to his local pastor and also to a chosen few intercessors who pray daily for him and his family as well as for his business affairs.

CHAPTER 9: MATURITY AND DISCIPLINE

I have studied Dave's life and business practices for more than five years and also done a number of recordings with him and the people he surrounds himself with. It has been heartening to discover a disciplined life of someone who truly is Kingdom-minded and a disciple of Christ.

Jordan Peterson — Psychologist Speaking Truth to a Generation

> "If I want to be great I have to win the victory over myself [...] Self-discipline."
>
> — Harry S. Truman

The final person who has impacted my life by their amazing discipline is Jordan Peterson, a University of Toronto professor. He does not necessarily approach life from a traditional Christian perspective, but his ideas and lectures should challenge every Christian believer. Peterson comes at life from a psychology angle, and he has put an enormous amount of thought and study into the human condition and into the writings of some of the greatest minds in the past 200–300 years of human endeavor.

In 1999, Peterson released a book called *Maps of Meaning: The Architecture of Belief* and it documents how human beings create meaning for their lives. The book took 13 years to write, and Peterson says he spent about three hours a day on this one book. He says that EVERY sentence in that 576-page book was written and then rewritten over 50 times. Peterson is so careful with his words and so accurate in what he says and how he says it, that many of his critics have had a very difficult time finding ammunition against his ideas. Peterson represents to me someone who is very mature in his life and in his calling. Although not advocating a born-again experience, he deeply believes in the validity of Scripture and says truthful communication has to be at the foundation of every human interaction. His grasp of Scripture and of the plight of human existence often make me think that deep down, he has a genuine relationship with Christ.

In a more recent book, *12 Rules for Life An Antidote to Chaos*, Peterson has taken his ideas for life and living mainstream. He has been packing out auditoriums, frequently with 3,000–5,000 people in each of his appearances. Many of those attending are young adults with serious questions about the meaning of life. Peterson talks about the tension in all of life between order and chaos, and his combination of practical wisdom based largely on biblical values and the archetypes promoted by Carl Jung is striking a huge chord with a very broad spectrum of people. Peterson has put over 500 hours of his lectures on YouTube®, and his content continues to generate hundreds of millions of views.

Why do I respect Peterson so much? It's because he took more than 30 years of disciplined reading, study, teaching, and writing to mature his understanding of human psychology and of human behavior. It's because he foundationally has a profound understanding of truth and of Jesus being the *Logos*, the one who lived truth to its fullest capacity. Although I don't agree with all of Peterson's conclusions or ideas, I have to respect his scholarship, his discipline, his principled positions and his mature ability to articulate his ideas to an often hostile and politically correct world. I recommend that people listen to Peterson's lectures and interviews on YouTube and social media, and I put him forward as an example of a mature voice in the marketplace of ideas. He is extremely intentional about all of his words and his actions. He is precise in his use of language, and in the meaning, he conveys in every sentence he speaks or writes. His lifestyle inspires me to do better in all these areas.

Intentionality and Human Will

> "Commitment is doing the thing you said you would do,
> long after the mood you said it in has left you!"
>
> — George Zalucki

I once heard John Bevere asked about how he was able to write so many books. His answer surprised me. He said he created a discipline of not going into the office until he had written 1,000 words. If you do 1,000 words each day, it is not long until you have a full book. Discipline involves the WILL of a human being. Consider the use of the words "I will" in Psalm 101, which King David wrote:

1. **I will** sing of mercy and justice;
   To You, O LORD, **I will** sing praises.
2. **I will** behave wisely in a perfect way.
   Oh, when will you come to me?
   I will walk within my house with a perfect heart
3. **I will** set nothing wicked before my eyes;

In another Psalm, David again penned these famous words: *This is the day the LORD has made,* ***we will*** *rejoice and be glad in it* (Psalms 118:24 NKJV).

When it comes to discipline, our WILL is one of our greatest weapons. In Paul's first letter to his spiritual son Timothy, he compares our walk with God to an athlete, a farmer, and a soldier. All three of these professions take an enormous amount of discipline. He also makes this very insightful statement about his OWN discipline, again comparing his preparation to an athlete:

> So I run with purpose in every step. I am not just shadowboxing. I discipline my body like an athlete, training it to do what it should. Otherwise, I fear that after preaching to others I myself might be disqualified (1 Corinthians 9:26-27 NLT).

We do have the capacity to exercise our human will over our endeavors, our behavior, and our attitude. Self-control is ALSO a fruit of the Holy Spirit, so hopefully the closer we walk with God, the easier discipline will be in our lives.

My Personal Disciplines
Like I said in my opening to this chapter, I am still on the journey to conquering in many areas of discipline. It is much easier sometimes NOT to be disciplined in many areas of our lives. The more mature we get, however, the more disciplined we should become. One thing I have learned to do is to set up certain disciplined PRACTICES that help keep me on track, literally like the rails of a train.

One of those is a non-negotiable time of prayer that starts our work at Good Shepherd Ministries, International. I PAY people to be there and start the day with prayer. We spend the first half an hour of EVERY day at work in prayer for our partners, for requests that have been sent to us from hurting people, for upcoming missions, projects, and endeavors, for each other and most often for finances and provision. We must be doing something right because, although our expenses are HUGE (over $40,000 per week), we have NEVER missed a payroll and we pay our bills on time.

Secondly, I set strict disciplines of operation in my office. We pay bills every Friday, payroll every second Thursday, commissions on the 11th of each month and giving to other ministries on the 22nd of each month. Every morning I get about four reports of income streams into the ministry through wires, online giving, online sales, and physical mail. In the evening I always get an end of day report, starting with the previous day's balance and showing ALL incoming and outgoing flows of finances and showing me an exact end-of-day. I also see a budget sheet every two weeks at payroll time to determine from where funds can be taken. In addition, we now map out a production schedule for every month in advance showing recordings, communications, and social media campaigns and postings.

Whenever a designated gift is given, it is NEVER shown as a part of our bottom line because I make myself blind to it. It can and should ONLY be used for the purpose it has been given, so it does not appear except on a budget sheet showing designated funds. When we receive funds designated for degrees or other ministries, those funds are separated at the point of receipt so they will NOT be touched for other purposes. These disciplines have held us in good stead for decades and have greatly helped us stay on track and maintain a high level of ministry integrity.

The principle here is to create systems that provide a structure for discipline to function in. It is so hard to accomplish anything in our lives without some vehicle of process, some plan, something that has goals and requirements. We as human beings actually NEED such structures in order to become disciplined. When we are younger, school, sports coaches, teachers, and administrators impose most of those structures upon us. To some degree the government and businesses take over from there but, when it comes to our relationship with God, we have to set those systems into place personally.

There are two areas of spiritual process in which God has helped me to have solid discipline. One is in the reading of His Word and the second is prayer. When it comes to Bible reading, I follow a plan by Craig Groeschel's YouVersion®. It is the Tyndale One Year® Bible Reading Plan, and it provides a balanced reading each day from Old and New Testaments plus a Psalms reading and a Proverbs reading.

You can invite up to 150 other people to participate with you in the plan, and if you simply follow the readings, in one year you will read through the entire Bible. Each day, there is a place where anyone can comment on the reading, and that is shared with the group. I'm on my fifth year in a row of reading the Bible through in a year, and it's a very healthy discipline in my daily walk with God. It also provides a great mentoring tool that enables you to help those you are discipling and gives you tangible Scripture to interact over every day.

It just so happens that I am writing this chapter on January 1, 2019, and today's reading began with Genesis1 and 2, plus Matthew 1, Psalms 1:1–6 and Proverbs 1:1–6. In today's six verses the word DISCIPLINE comes up TWICE.

1 These are the proverbs of Solomon, David's son, king of Israel:
2 Their PURPOSE is to teach people wisdom and **discipline**, to help them understand the insights of the wise.

3		Their PURPOSE is to teach people to live **disciplined** and successful lives, to help them do what is right, just, and fair.
4		These proverbs will give insight to the simple, knowledge and discernment to the young.
5		Let the wise listen to these proverbs and become even wiser. Let those with understanding receive guidance
6		by exploring the meaning in these proverbs and parables, the words of the wise and their riddles.

Here is the comment I made: "These opening few verses on the PURPOSE of the Proverbs are very cool. They help people become disciplined and successful and help young people to become wise. I think wise sayings are awesome and I collect modern ones. I have about 50 in my new book coming out in February."

My Personal Prayer Life
The final area of discipline God has helped me cultivate is prayer. When I was younger, I used to go out into the night and spend hours in prayer. God taught me so much how to connect with him and how to have a structured time of prayer that took me into His presence and also accomplished prayer purposes outlined in His Word. These days I tend to wake up at about 5:30 a.m. and pace my living room floor. This seems to accomplish the same without the distractions of the great outdoors. I want to lay out my prayer structure as an example. There is nothing sacred about my pattern, but it may be helpful to others because many people borrow ideas from others who have been doing things longer in the LORD.

I always start with the Lord's Prayer because it is given to us by Jesus Himself as a pattern for prayer. I think about each sentence in that prayer as I pray it and use it to prepare my heart before God. I do think there is a reason we pray God will not lead us into temptation and that He would deliver us from evil. Although these are promises in the Bible, Jesus deemed it necessary that we SHOULD pray daily for these two protections to our lives.

As soon as I finish the Lord's Prayer, I submit myself to God and FORGIVE anyone who has sinned against me. I actually have a fairly long list of those who have wronged me over the years, and I forgive any who may still bother me. I will keep forgiving them until they no longer bother me. After I forgive others, I immediately ask the Father to forgive my sins by the blood of Jesus. The Lord's Prayer specifically lets us know that if we forgive others, then God will immediately forgive us.

As soon as I know my sins are confessed and forgiven, I go into warfare against the enemy. I bind the devil from my family, my home, my work, my finances and any part of my life. I submit myself to God and resist him and command him to flee according to James 4:7. This can take a few minutes because I often feel like I am warring in the spirit realm against demonic influences that seem to creep into areas of our lives each and every day. I will often sense a 'leaving' of those entities and a clarity of thought suddenly happening after they go. I then immediately ask God to cover my life, my home, my family and my work with the blood of Jesus. I ask Him to give His angels charge over me according to Psalms 91, and I ask that Jesus would dwell in my heart by faith according to Ephesians 3:17. I ask Him for the Holy Spirit according to Luke 11:13.

The prayer time goes into a much easier place after that supplication is over. I then pray three Scripture blessings over my life and family. These are:

The Moses prayer of blessing:

> "So you shall serve the LORD your God, **and** He will **bless** your **bread and** your **water. And** I will take sickness away from the midst of you (Exodus 23:25 NKJV).

The Jabez prayer of blessing:

> And **Jabez** called on the God of Israel saying, "Oh, that You would bless me indeed, and enlarge my territory, that Your hand would be with me, and that You would keep me from evil, that I may not cause pain!" So God granted him what he requested (1 Chronicles 4:10 NKJV).

The Abraham Promise, which my whole first book is about. According to Galatians 3:29, we as Christians are the 'seed' of Abraham:

> That in blessing I will bless thee, and in multiplying I will multiply thy seed as the stars of the heaven, and as the sand which is upon the sea shore; and thy seed shall possess the gate of his enemies; And in thy seed shall all the nations of the earth be blessed; because thou hast obeyed my voice (Genesis 22:17–18 KJV).

From there I go into praying for kings and those in authority, for our national and local leaders according to Paul's instruction to Timothy:

> I urge you, first of all, to pray for all people. Ask God to help them; intercede on their behalf, and give thanks for them. Pray this way for kings and all who are in authority so that we can live peaceful and quiet lives marked by godliness and dignity. This is good and pleases God our Savior (2 Timothy 2:1-3 NLT).

I then pray for Israel, for the peace of Jerusalem and for God's end-time purposes for that country. This is based on Psalms 122:6 and Isaiah 62:7

Then I pray specifically for my intimate family each by name, including my kids and their families, my mom, her husband and those in my family who are not yet committed to Christ.

Finally, I pray for friends, my ministry team, the people who I disciple and those close to my heart.

I end up praying three prayers over my prayer list. These are all prayers Paul prayed over people in the churches he covered. They are Ephesians 1:15–22, Ephesians 3:14–19 and Colossians 1:9–14.

This may seem like a lot, but every prayer is based in Scripture and really enables me to partner with the things God asks us to pray for. After I complete as much of this each day as I can, I often really feel God's presence and sense a strong guidance and grace throughout the day. It is also very easy throughout the day to pray in the Holy Spirit, in that wonderful prayer language God has given us as Christians to pray in. Your prayer time may look a lot different, but I do challenge you to create a structure to your time of prayer with God and get some Scripture and patterns that help you stay on track.

I can share in these areas of prayer, ministry management, and Bible reading because those disciplines are mature in my life. When it comes to exercise, perfect eating habits, depth of worship and a host of other areas, I am still pressing towards a mark that others I respect are setting. This area of discipline is one we hopefully are all maturing in, and the need to grow in it is a continual personal challenge. There is no question as to what the objective is. We all are supposed to be dying daily to self, to be putting the flesh under subjection to God's Spirit and to be holy, godly and reverent in our conduct. If there is one person who exemplified this type of selfless living in our generation, it has to be Mother Teresa. I think it is fitting that we close out this chapter with her 'Humility List.' Here it is:

Mother Teresa's Humility List

1. Speak as little as possible about yourself.
2. Keep busy with your own affairs and not those of others.
3. Avoid curiosity.
4. Do not interfere in the affairs of others.
5. Accept small irritations with good humor.
6. Do not dwell on the faults of others.
7. Accept censures even if unmerited.
8. Give in to the will of others.
9. Accept insults and injuries.
10. Accept contempt, being forgotten and disregarded.
11. Be courteous and delicate even when provoked by someone.
12. Do not seek to be admired and loved.
13. Do not protect yourself behind your own dignity.
14. Give in, in discussions, even when you are right.
15. Choose always the more difficult task.

If those 15 points are not convicting, you probably don't have a pulse. I pray that some of what I have shared in this chapter will be inspirational and helpful to at least give a target to aim at when it comes to personal discipline.

CHAPTER TEN

Maturity and Truth

Jesus said to the people who believed in him, "You are truly my disciples if you remain faithful to my teachings. And you will know the truth, and the truth will set you free.

— John 8:31 NLT

"If the truth isn't enough, then you must become stronger at presenting it."

— Jim Rohn

Truth is what most accurately reflects God's perspective on any given topic. Jesus in Matthew 16 asked His disciples who people said He was. They gave Him a variety of opinions, and I am sure each opinion was well reasoned and had some valid justifications, but it did not mean every opinion was "truth." Jesus then turned to Peter and asked him the same questions. Peter answered, *"Thou art the Christ, the Son of the Living God."* The response Jesus gave to Peter was very revealing. *"Blessed are you Simon Barjonah, for flesh and blood did not reveal this to you but my Father in heaven."* What Jesus was saying was that revealed "truth" from the Father trumped all opinions and that what Peter understood was the "truth" about Jesus' identity.

Now it is interesting that just six verses later, Jesus says to the same Peter, *"Get behind me Satan,"* in response to Peter trying to dissuade Jesus not to go to the cross. You see Peter had a revelation of "truth" concerning who Jesus was but Peter did not have a revelation of what Jesus was supposed to do and accomplish on the earth. We must understand that just because someone understands one area of "truth," does not mean they necessarily understand other areas of "truth." Truth in our own lives and in others must be continually discerned.

In a previous chapter, I wrote about Nelson Mandela. He came from the Xhosa tribe in South Africa, one that has gained a lot of interest due to the global influence Mandela has had. What most people don't know is that the entire Xhosa nation came close to being wiped out by a single lie in the middle of the 19th century. James Michener documents the story in his epic book on South Africa called *The Covenant*. He tells how in 1856, a 14 year old Xhosa girl by the name of Norgqause, went into a trance and gave a prophecy that if the Xhosa tribes would kill their livestock and destroy all their crops, that on a certain day the Russians would arrive by sea on the Xhosa beaches and rescue the nation from the advancing white settlers. Her uncle Mhlakaze, a nefarious visionary seer, set that day as February 18th, 1857.

Tragically the whole nation decided to obey the terms of the prophecy, and they killed all their livestock and destroyed all their crops. On February 18th, 1857 the whole tribe gathered on the beaches looking for Russian ships to magically appear on the horizon. As night fell and no deliverance came, a whole nation began to understand that they had believed a lie and that tens of thousands of people were going to perish in the ensuing months as a result of starvation. It's a miracle that the lineage of Mandela survived this awful tragedy. It is vital that we believe truth and not error as what we believe will determine our actions and will impact our destiny.

You cannot separate truth from maturity. Some people's understanding is simply sincerely wrong. Before his Damascus Road conversion, Saul (later Paul) was sincerely wrong about who he thought Christians were. Only a face-to-face encounter with the risen Christ changed his mind and caused him to embrace the "truth" about the Gospel. Before the Apostle Peter had his Acts 10 experience in the house of the Roman centurion Cornelius, he was completely wrong in his understanding concerning the access of Christianity to the Gentile world. The greatest prisons people often get themselves to involve believing the wrong things about themselves and about others.

Harold Houdini
I heard an amazing story about the greatest escape artist of the last century, Harold Houdini. It was said that he had the ability to escape any chain, lock or imprisonment. They say Houdini could ingest a lock-picking device and regurgitate it in a moment into his mouth, and gripping it with his teeth, was able to open virtually any lock. In fact, prisons would use Houdini to test the security of their prison cells and, time and again, he was able to break free.

But the story I heard spoke of the ONE time that Houdini was unable to break out of a prison cell. It was in southern Italy, and he tried everything he knew for a period of three hours to get free from the cell they had put him in. For the first time, he capitulated and admitted that the secret to getting out of this cell had eluded him and he gave up. The reason this specific cell was unable to be unlocked was that it was ALREADY OPEN. They HAD NEVER LOCKED IT.

Houdini could have walked out of that cell in a moment, but he didn't because he was trapped in the prison of his own mind and in his wrong perception of his situation. This is such a picture of Christians today, and this is the reason Jesus said: "*the truth shall make you free.*" The path to freedom and victory in life is through "revealed truth." This is also the pathway to maturity. In the light of this principle the words of Jesus in John 8:31 make a lot more sense: "*If you abide in My word, you are My disciples indeed. And you shall know the truth, and the truth shall make you free.*"

The Emmaus Road

My first book *Unlocking the Abraham Promise* taught extensively about 1 Corinthians 3:6 where Paul writes *"I planted, Apollos watered, but God gave the increase."* The role of Apollos was highlighted as being the role of the "teacher," and specifically the Bible says in Acts 18 that Apollos taught accurately the things of the LORD. I contend that God only builds His Church on the revealed "truth" of His Word. It's not just information or opinion that will move people to maturity, it's when flesh and blood did not show things to a person, but rather they had a direct download from heaven.

An interesting study can be done concerning the interaction between Jesus and His disciples on the day of the resurrection as recorded in the book of Luke. Jesus first meets up with two of them on the road to Emmaus, where He walks with them but does not allow them to perceive who He is. They are depressed and confused by the recent crucifixion and burial of Christ. Jesus first acts as though He doesn't know what had happened but then admonishes them for being so slow to believe. He says, *"Oh foolish ones, and slow of heart to believe in all that the prophets have spoken! Ought not the Christ to have suffered these things and to enter into His glory?"* Jesus then begins to explain the Scriptures to them. Luke describes it like this: *"And beginning at Moses and all the Prophets, He expounded to them in ALL the Scriptures the things concerning Himself"* (Luke 24:25-27 NKJV).

They stopped at a village, and Jesus joined them for a meal. He took bread, blessed and broke it, and gave it to them. The Bible says in the next verse, *"Then their eyes were opened and they knew Him; and He vanished from their sight"* (Luke 24:31 NKJV). The amazing thing in this whole chapter is how God is able to open and close our eyes to truth and to Himself. Jesus, working with the Holy Spirit, is the greatest truth revealer and truth concealer that there is. After they recognized Him, He disappeared, and they then discussed the Scripture "truth" Jesus had revealed to them. Here is how they described the experience: *"Did not our heart burn within us while He talked with us on the road, and while He opened the Scriptures to us"* (Luke 24:32 NKJV).

If you follow this final chapter of Luke's Gospel to the end, you see how much Jesus opens and closes eyes. The disciples hurry back to the 11 apostles and other disciples in Jerusalem, and while they are gathered together, Jesus appears to them again. He openly shows them His hands and His feet and even eats some fish and honeycomb in front of them. Then in Luke 24:45 it says the following: **"And He opened their understanding, that they might comprehend the Scriptures."** Finally, Jesus reveals the purpose of it all, *"That repentance and remission of sins should be preached in His Name to all nations, beginning at Jerusalem."* Jesus then gives them instructions to wait in Jerusalem until the gift of the Holy Spirit is poured out upon them.

In this one chapter, Jesus opened their eyes to Scriptural history that prophesied His time on earth. He revealed Himself in that present time to His disciples, and He revealed the purpose and destiny of the Church for the future. It was one eye-opening revelation after another, the past, the present, and the future, all in that one chapter of Luke 24.

Scripture "truth," when shared and revealed by someone who has a revelation of it, will cause our hearts to burn as the Holy Spirit bears witness to our spirit that the understanding and the wisdom is from God. It's a wonderful experience when this happens because "truth" carries with it authority and an anointing from God. This is why I am so passionate about revelation teaching. I search around the world for those who carry it in different areas. When I discover it, I often feel like I need to go on a quest to capture it, translate it and find a way to deliver it to the Body of Christ worldwide.

Revelation Teaching
One example is that series we recorded in the Philippines titled *Navigating Betrayal* by David Sumrall, nephew of the famous Lester Sumrall. I briefly mentioned this recording earlier in the book when dealing with how people change and the dangers of success. The genesis of that unique and powerful recording went back to a graduation I did in Bondi Beach outside Sydney, Australia. The pastor of the church where I was preaching, Mark Horan, handed me two CDs on the subject of betrayal before I returned back to the USA. Flying back on the plane, I listened to the teaching and discerned a man who had been deeply wounded by betrayal but had used that experience to get wisdom from God as to how to get through the difficult process and find healing and understanding on the other side.

When I arrived back in California, I worked to get in touch with David Sumrall in Manila. He was quite cold to American ministries, thinking they only wanted to exploit him for money. I pushed my credentials as being from Africa and of being a friend of his friend in Australia. He finally agreed to record with us for three hours. I literally flew my camera crew over to the Philippines to capture these messages. I was willing to take ANY restrictions he chose to put on our recording team. Yet, when David saw our hearts, we became friends, and I spent the next day with him in Hong Kong. The two sessions we captured on *Navigating Betrayal* have helped countless families and so many people. The ISOM program that we have been developing for decades is nothing more than a gathering of revelation teaching from some of God's finest instructors. When people go through one revelation teacher after another, they find their hearts burning within them, and their understanding is enlightened. The life transformation in ISOM schools globally is tangible, and tens of thousands of students and pastors can attest to it. If you go through a year of teaching with back to back instructors like Reinhard Bonnke, John Bevere, Joyce Meyer, Bill Winston, Marilyn Hickey, Jack Hayford, Brian Houston, A.R. Bernard, T.L. Osborn, and others, and you are not impacted or transformed, then I contend you need help. Revealed "truth" will make your heart burn, will change you, and correctly align your thinking and understanding.

Proverbs 20:5 talks about this concept of people carrying deep understanding. It says, *"Counsel in the heart of man is like deep water, But a man of understanding will draw it out."* When the different speakers came to record for our ISOM program, many of them asked me what I wanted them to teach on. Some had written dozens of books and knew a lot about many topics. My favorite response to many of these teachers was, "If you knew that this was your last week on earth and you had ONE last chance to leave behind the most important message that God has given you for the global Church, that is the message I want you to teach on."

I also told the teachers to not only teach the knowledge and understanding of their distinctive messages but to pray at the conclusion of their teaching that there would be an impartation of the anointing or grace from their lives into the lives of those being taught. The testimonies we have received from around the world of miracles, healings and life transformation through those prayers have been remarkable.

Metamorphosis
I truly believe that Paul in Romans 12:2 is referring to this process of discovering your calling and being changed into the image of Christ through revelation TRUTH. I like the way the New Living Translation puts it:

> Don't copy the behavior and customs of this world, but let God **transform you** into a new person by **changing the way you think**. Then you will learn to **know God's will for you**, which is good and pleasing and perfect (Romans 12:2 NLT).

It is obvious from this Scripture that correct knowledge of God's TRUTH changes your thinking. The word *transform* here is the same root word used in the Greek to talk about the metamorphosis or transformation of a pupa into a butterfly. There is a radical transformation that happens in the life of a believer through the changing of their THINKING and that change happens through the revelation understanding of God's Word. The interesting consequence is that a believer will come to "know God's will for you" which indicates that a person's understanding of their CALLING will come out of this "thinking transformation."

The Importance of the Five-fold Ministry
When it comes to the maturing process, you cannot get away from "revealed truth" being taught by people who carry revelation understanding in their areas of expertise. Each teacher you draw from has to stay in their own lane and not teach outside of their areas of revelation. In the light of what we have learned in this chapter about "revealed truth" being taught by those who understand, let's examine the famous verses on maturity and the five-fold ministry in Ephesians 4:

> Now these are the gifts Christ gave to the church: the apostles, the prophets, the evangelists, and the pastors and teachers. Their responsibility is to equip God's people to do his work and build up the church, the body of Christ. This will continue until we all come to such unity in our faith and knowledge of God's Son that we will be **mature in the Lord**, measuring up to the full and complete standard of Christ. Then **we will no longer be immature like children**. We won't be tossed and blown about by every wind of new teaching. We will not be influenced when people try to trick us with lies so clever they sound like the truth. Instead, we will speak the truth in love, growing in every way more and more like Christ, who is the head of his body, the church. He makes the whole body fit together perfectly. As each part does its own special work, it helps the other parts grow, so that the whole body is healthy and growing and full of love
> (Ephesians 4:11-16 NLT).

This Scripture reveals an incredible insight into the maturing process. First of all, it is a critical reason why EVERY church needs to recognize the importance of equipping their members with a balanced input of ALL of the five-fold gifts. These gifts mentioned here by Paul in Ephesians are the pastor, the teacher, the apostle, the evangelist, and the prophet. Many churches teach that the apostle and prophet are not needed so much today, but that is simply not true.

It is important to understand that nobody has all "revealed truth" except God. We need revelation from different parts of His leadership and His Church if we are to mature in a balanced and healthy way. Each revelation reveals a new sparkling facet in God's amazing diamond of truth.

This is the reason we drew on mature five-fold teachers in the ISOM to help each church equip their believers. We understood that many young congregations, especially in foreign developing nations, may not have mature apostles or prophets or even teachers. Understanding this incredible Scripture in Ephesians 4, we knew we had to capture those giftings via video and help bring them to both churches and individuals in the nations. The results of over 30 different instructors teaching believers in the first two years of the ISOM program is amazing growth and deep maturity beginning to happen in both the individual believers and in the life of the church.

The second part of this Ephesians 4 Scripture is the following: *"This* (the equipping by five-fold ministers) *will continue until we all come to such **unity in our faith and knowledge of God's Son** that we will be **mature in the LORD**, measuring up to the full and complete standard of Christ"* (Ephesians 4:13 NLT).

Again we see the importance of **knowledge** being given to Christians through being equipped by five-fold ministry teachers. This will result in two objectives being accomplished in the life of a believer, the faith of many believers being knit together into ONE unity through such an equipping and each believer coming into a true **knowledge** of God's Son. The end result Paul writes is that *"we will be **mature in the LORD**, measuring up to the full and complete standard of Christ."* Wow, what an insight and what an understanding of the process of becoming mature.

I cannot see how local churches will EVER bring their members to maturity without understanding this Ephesians 4 Scripture. I am not saying the ISOM is the only way to accomplish this, but I am saying that church leaders need to understand the importance on drawing on mature five-fold graces in the global Church to equip their members so they will become unified in their faith and gain a deep knowledge of Jesus Christ as God's Son. These two elements brought about by such an equipping will contribute greatly to the maturity of their congregation members.

Paul, in this Ephesian 4 Scripture, is not done explaining the benefits of such equipping. He now moves into the area of stabilizing the faith of believers. Probably my greatest frustration as a young believer was how much of a yoyo my faith was. I would experience wonderful worship in a fellowship service and be touched by God's power. I would go to bed so full of God's joy and love only to wake up the next morning feeling like a truck had rolled over me in the night. I actually asked my leaders how it was that I could "leak" so much in the night and feel so different the next day. I would then often wrestle with doubts and condemnation all through the week until the next time I could get a spiritual "high."

Paul says that a part of the maturing process happens through teaching from five-fold teachers and indicates that the following result would happen to those who are taught:

> Then **we will no longer be immature like children**. We won't be tossed and blown about by every wind of new teaching. We will not be influenced when people try to trick us with lies so clever they sound like the truth. Instead, we will speak the truth in love, growing in every way more and more like Christ, who is the head of his body, the church. He makes the whole body fit together perfectly. As each part does its own special work, it helps the other parts grow, so that the whole body is healthy and growing and full of love (Ephesians 4:14-16 NLT).

Growing up to be like Jesus is what it is ALL about. If there is ANY proof Scripture in the WHOLE Bible about this process of maturity, this Ephesians 4:11-16 is it. In a later chapter, I will deal more specifically with this issue of stability and balance. It is a HUGE part of becoming mature. What I do want to emphasize through the last part of this Scripture is the importance of TRUTH in the equation of maturity. One of the things Paul warned the Ephesian believers about was error destroying them. When Paul said farewell to the Ephesian elders in Acts 20, this is what he said:

> "I declare today that I have been faithful. If anyone suffers eternal death, it's not my fault, for I didn't shrink from declaring all that God wants you to know So **guard yourselves** and God's people. Feed and shepherd God's flock—his church, purchased with his own blood—over which the Holy Spirit has appointed you as leaders. I know that **false teachers**, like vicious wolves, will come in among you after I leave, not sparing the flock. Even some men from your own group will rise up and **distort the truth** in order to draw a following. Watch out! Remember the three years I was with you—my constant watch and care over you night and day, and my many tears for you. And now I entrust you to God and the message of his grace that is able to build you up and give you an inheritance with all those he has set apart for himself" (Acts 20:26-32 NKJV).

At the heart of Paul's plea here is for believers NOT to be deceived by teaching that was FALSE. I have highlighted the words **guard yourselves, false teachers**, and **distort the truth**. Truth is at the heart of a person's salvation and **growing up** or **maturing** in truth means also not becoming trapped by lies and false teaching. I love the quote by Lisa Bevere, which I often tweet out, it is simply this: "What Satan cannot prevent, he perverts."

Teaching people to discern truth and error is so valuable in God's Kingdom. This is one of the reasons we draw on mature ministry leaders to teach in the ISOM. We try to find instructors with dozens of years of integrity and fruit. We look for a specific revelation understanding that we discern to be mature and then we test it, often for years, before we settle on endorsing it. Sometimes we have had to remove content or a specific session because we felt it went outside of our standards. As much as possible we try to provide churches and individuals with distilled truth from mature five-fold ministry teachers to help in this Ephesians 4 maturing process.

We know that after Paul, Timothy took the pastoral responsibility of the Ephesian church. The many admonitions by the Apostle Paul to Timothy concerning his pastoral work can be found in the two letters Paul penned to Timothy, the second being from prison. If there is one common theme in those two letters, it was a warning against **false teaching** and **false people**. Please notice how many times Paul talks about **teaching** and **truth**. Here is an incredible list of such admonitions by Paul to Timothy from those two letters:

- When I left for Macedonia, I urged you to stay there in Ephesus and stop those whose teaching is contrary to the truth (1 Timothy 1:3 NLT).

- Now the Holy Spirit tells us clearly that in the last times some will turn away from the true faith; they will follow deceptive spirits and teachings that come from demons (1 Timothy 4:1 NLT).

- Teach these things and insist that everyone learn them. Don't let anyone think less of you because you are young. Be an example to all believers in what you say, in the way you live, in your love, your faith, and your purity. Until I get there, focus on reading the Scriptures to the church, encouraging the believers, and teaching them. (1 Timothy 4:11–13 NLT).

- Keep a close watch on how you live and on your teaching. Stay true to what is right for the sake of your own salvation and the salvation of those who hear you. (1 Timothy 4:16 NLT).

- Teach these things, Timothy, and encourage everyone to obey them. Some people may contradict our teaching, but these are the wholesome teachings of the LORD Jesus Christ. These teachings promote a godly life. Anyone who teaches something different is arrogant and lacks understanding (1 Timothy 6:2-4 NLT).

- Timothy, guard what God has entrusted to you. Avoid godless, foolish discussions with those who oppose you with their so-called knowledge. Some people have wandered from the faith by following such foolishness (1 Timothy 6:20-21 NLT).

- Hold on to the pattern of wholesome teaching you learned from me—a pattern shaped by the faith and love that you have in Christ Jesus. Through the power of the Holy Spirit who lives within us, carefully guard the precious truth that has been entrusted to you (2 Timothy 1:13-14 NLT).

- You have heard me teach things that have been confirmed by many reliable witnesses. Now teach these truths to other trustworthy people who will be able to pass them on to others. (2 Timothy 2:2 NLT).

- Work hard so you can present yourself to God and receive his approval. Be a good worker, one who does not need to be ashamed and who correctly explains the word of truth. Avoid worthless, foolish talk that only leads to more godless behavior. This kind of talk spreads like cancer (2 Timothy 2:15-17 NLT).

- Gently instruct those who oppose the truth. Perhaps God will change those people's hearts, and they will learn the truth. Then they will come to their senses and escape from the devil's trap. For they have been held captive by him to do whatever he wants (2 Timothy 2:25-26 NLT).

- But you must remain faithful to the things you have been taught. You know they are true, for you know you can trust those who taught you. You have been taught the holy Scriptures from childhood, and they have given you the wisdom to receive the salvation that comes by trusting in Christ Jesus. All Scripture is inspired by God and is useful to teach us what is true and to make us realize what is wrong in our lives. It corrects us when we are wrong and teaches us to do what is right. God uses it to prepare and equip his people to do every good work (2 Timothy 3:14–17 NLT).

- I solemnly urge you in the presence of God and Christ Jesus, who will someday judge the living and the dead when he comes to set up his Kingdom: Preach the word of God. Be prepared, whether the time is favorable or not. Patiently correct, rebuke, and encourage your people with good teaching. For a time is coming when people will no longer listen to sound and wholesome teaching. They will follow their own desires and will look for teachers who will tell them whatever their itching ears want to hear. They will reject the truth and chase after myths (2 Timothy 4:1–4 NLT).

We have learned in this chapter that "revealed truth" delivers people from the bondage of lies. It DOES matter what we believe. Not all teaching is truth and just because people are SINCERE, doesn't make them RIGHT. A person like Saul before he converted was VERY SINCERE and passionate and zealous and convincing. He was SINCERELY WRONG. Truth must be continually discerned, and we need to know the truth by its fruit in our lives and in the lives of others.

So to conclude this chapter, let me summarize. In order for believers to mature in a healthy way, they need to be TAUGHT revelation TRUTH from different five-fold ministry gifts of Christ's leadership and His Church. Each revelation they learn unfolds to them a new sparkling facet in God's amazing diamond of truth. All effort must be made to prevent God's people from believing a lie, and only true revelation will make people free and keep them free. What I want to show in the next chapter is a fascinating and intriguing example of how to mine TRUTH from God's Word.

CHAPTER ELEVEN

How to Mine Truth: Pilate and the Crucifixion

A major quality of maturity is the ability to examine all facets of a biblical passage or story and to extract truth and a right perspective and understanding from it. A mature judge will hear all sides of a case before passing judgment. The more a judge understands all facets of a crime, the more mature, fair and right their judgment will be. So many Christians only read the Bible in a surface way and miss so much truth.

Growing up in Johannesburg, South Africa, I was exposed a lot to gold mining, and the mining dumps were literally the landmarks that were all over that city. One of the aspects that fascinated me about gold mining was how those seeking to discover and extract it were mostly looking for a gold vein in the rock. In parts of the world like Argentina, these veins can go for miles. Mining companies look for low distortions in the magnetic fields coming from a rocky terrain. This enables them to find faults in the rock, which are often places that can be mined and gold discovered. Once discovering a gold vein, these mining companies will often mine down the vein to extract as much gold as possible from that deposit.

When it comes to truth in the Scriptures, we all need to learn to mine down the vein. Very often we will discover a truth but often get only a small amount of benefit from that truth because we are unwilling to mine it. Mining down a Scriptural vein means viewing a topic from multiple angles, looking at the context and personalities involved in a story, looking at the mindset of the people and the historical background to a story. While working on this book, I felt God showed me a fascinating study that involved primarily the character and person of Pontius Pilate. As an exercise in a mature reading of a critical Bible character and event, we are going to examine the person of Pontius Pilate and his judgment concerning the crucifixion of Jesus in the New Testament. We have four accounts, all seeing this event from different perspectives. I think you will be amazed to discover the truth about this very misunderstood event. I believe after you read the pages that follow, that you will see the personality of Pilate and the event of the crucifixion in an entirely different light. This study will also hopefully inspire you to mine many other portions of Scripture to extract precious nuggets of truth that will enrich your life.

Jesus before Annas

Let's make sure we get the timeline correct. After Jesus was arrested in the Garden of Gethsemane, he was taken to the house of Annas, the father in law of Caiaphas. According to historians, Annas had been the high priest from AD 6–15, but he had been removed from power by the Romans. He, however, still exercised significant power behind the scenes. Although not sanctioned by the Romans, he nonetheless was still considered to be functioning in that high priest capacity by the Jews. It is interesting to note that Luke 3:1–2 (NKJV) says:

> Now in the fifteenth year of the reign of Tiberius Caesar, Pontius Pilate being governor of Judea, Herod being tetrarch of Galilee, his brother Philip tetrarch of Iturea and the region of Trachonitis, and Lysanias tetrarch of Abilene, **while Annas and Caiaphas were high priests**, the word of God came to John the son of Zacharias in the wilderness.

So it is helpful to know that there are two people who are called the high priest in these chapters and knowing which one is being referred to can be a little tricky. Jesus is fairly responsive to Annas. John gives us some details:

> The high priest then asked Jesus about His disciples and His doctrine. Jesus answered him, "I spoke openly to the world. I always taught in synagogues and in the temple, where the Jews always meet, and in secret I have said nothing. Why do you ask Me? Ask those who have heard Me what I said to them. Indeed they know what I said." And when He had said these things, one of the officers who stood by struck Jesus with the palm of his hand, saying, "Do You answer the high priest like that?" Jesus answered him, "If I have spoken evil, bear witness of the evil; but if well, why do you strike Me?" Then Annas sent Him bound to Caiaphas the high priest (John 18:19–24 NKJV).

So here we get a record of the first physical strike against Jesus, probably a heavy slap across the face. It was to be followed by the first beating and mocking by the Temple guard. It is clear from the book of Luke that before Jesus got to Caiaphas' house, that Jesus was blindfolded, mocked and beaten by the Temple guard soldiers who held him. Here is how Luke described that second physical attack against Jesus, which took place at the house of Annas:

> Now the men who held Jesus mocked Him and beat Him. And having blindfolded Him, they struck Him on the face and asked Him, saying, "Prophesy! Who is the one who struck You?" And many other things they blasphemously spoke against Him (Luke 22:63–65 NKJV).

It is clear from Luke's account that this happened before Jesus got to the house of Caiaphas and before He had to face the full Sanhedrin. Jesus hadn't even gotten near to Pilate yet, and He is still at this point being pushed around and mistreated by the Temple guards and the Jewish leaders.

Jesus before Caiaphas
Jesus, in the early hours of the morning, is brought bound and beaten to the house of the official high priest, Caiaphas. Here Jesus refuses to respond to any of the questions or accusations that were put to him. This is how Matthew tells it:

> Now the chief priests, the elders, and all the council sought false testimony against Jesus to put Him to death, but found none. Even though many false witnesses came forward, they found none. But at last two false witnesses came forward and said, "This fellow said, 'I am able to destroy the temple of God and to build it in three days.'" And the high priest arose and said to Him, "Do You answer nothing? What is it these men testify against You?" But Jesus kept silent (Matthew 26:59–63 NKJV).

Jesus, first of all, refuses to answer his Sanhedrin accusers and doesn't say a word until the high priest puts Jesus under oath and extracts a statement of who He is from Him:

> And the high priest arose and said to Him, "Do You answer nothing? What is it these men testify against You?" But Jesus kept silent. And the high priest answered and said to Him, "**I put You under oath by the living God**: Tell us if You are the Christ, the Son of God!" Jesus said to him, "**It is as you said. Nevertheless, I say to you, hereafter you will see the Son of Man sitting at the right hand of the Power, and coming on the clouds of heaven.**" Then the high priest tore his clothes, saying, "He has spoken blasphemy! What further need do we have of witnesses? Look, now you have heard His blasphemy! What do you think?" They answered and said, "He is deserving of death" (Matthew 26:63–66 NKJV).

This statement made under oath provided the basis for the central case of the Sanhedrin against Jesus. This gathering of the chief priests, the elders, and all the counsel was going nowhere. Jesus had remained completely silent in the face of ridiculous, unproven and uncorroborated accusations until the high priest extracted this single statement from Jesus by putting Him under oath and forcing Him to reveal the truth about His identity.

Armed with this single piece of evidence, they were now going to approach Pilate to try and secure a death penalty ruling. Both Matthew and Mark say that after Caiaphas pronounced his judgment, that Jesus was subjected to a third physical beating. It is important to keep track of exactly how much abuse Jesus took because, at first reading, they all seem to blur together. I think Mark makes this third beating the clearest:

> Then the high priest tore his clothes and said, "What further need do we have of witnesses? You have heard the blasphemy! What do you think?" And they all condemned Him to be deserving of death. Then some began to spit on Him, and to blindfold Him, and to beat Him, and to say to Him, "Prophesy!" And the officers struck Him with the palms of their hands. (Mark 14:63–65 NKJV)

It is important to note that one other key thing happened at the house of Caiaphas. It was there that Peter denied Jesus three times and vehemently said that he did not even know Jesus. In one account, in Luke 22:60, it says that, right when his third denial happened, Jesus turned and looked at Peter:

> Then after about an hour had passed, another confidently affirmed, saying, "Surely this fellow also was with Him, for he is a Galilean." But Peter said, "Man, I do not know what you are saying!" Immediately, while he was still speaking, the rooster crowed. **And the Lord turned and looked at Peter**. Then Peter remembered the word of the Lord, how He had said to him, "Before the rooster crows, you will deny Me three times." So Peter went out and wept bitterly
> (Luke 22:59–62 NKJV).

So after being physically beaten three times and denied three times by one of his closest disciples, Jesus now, without sleep, has to face Pontius Pilate. He is taken bound from the house of Caiaphas, the high priest to the Roman Praetorium.

Jesus Before Pilate

When Jesus first stood before Pilate, He made this declaration *"for this cause I was born, and for this cause I have come into the world, that I should bear witness to the truth."* Pilate responded: *"What is truth?"* (John 18:37 NKJV)

I'm sure, in Pilate's mind, the lines between truth and error had gotten very blurry. Being a politician of Rome and posted to Jerusalem, I'm sure he constantly had to deal with riots and insurrection, military hierarchy, the zeal of the Jewish religious leadership and their contempt for Roman occupation. I'm sure that, most of the time, he was just trying to balance his loyalties to Rome with some sense of justice, but mindful that keeping the fragile peace and maintaining, as far as possible, the status quo was always the safest play. I'm sure Pilate was experienced and adept at making astute and expedient political and social decisions. Into his world suddenly steps Jesus.

Nothing about this prisoner from Nazareth fit any mold Pilate knew or understood. The man had committed no obvious crime, yet the rulers of the Jews were clamoring for the death penalty. The accusation used to justify putting him to death was supposedly their sudden newly found allegiance to Caesar and their feigned horror that any Jew might threaten Caesar's position by calling themselves a king. Hold on, these people hated Caesar and despised his rulership. Nothing about this case would have made sense to Pontius Pilate. He had been doing this long enough to know he did not have the full story, so he calls Jesus into the Praetorium to find out more.

Pilate's first conversation with Jesus is extremely interesting. In Matthew 27:11, Pilate flat out asks Jesus, *"Are you the King of the Jews?"* Jesus answers, *"It is as you say."* This exact response is affirmed in the Gospels of Mark (15:2) and in Luke 23:3. What is even more difficult to grasp is Pilate's response in Luke 23:4.

So Pilate said to the chief priests and the crowd, *"I find no fault in this man."* It's almost inconceivable that Pilate wouldn't care that a person under his jurisdiction was openly defying Rome and declaring Himself a king.

The Gospel of John provides a much more detailed understanding of this first interaction and why Pilate said what he did. Let's have John give us some context and then pull back the veil as to what really transpired here:

> Then they led Jesus from Caiaphas to the Praetorium, and it was early morning. But they themselves did not go into the Praetorium, lest they should be defiled, but that they might eat the Passover. Pilate then went out to them and said, "What accusation do you bring against this man?" They answered and said to him, "If he were not an evildoer, we would not have delivered Him up to you." Then Pilate said to them, "You take Him and judge Him according to your law." Therefore the Jews said to him, "It is not lawful for us to put anyone to death," that the saying of Jesus might be fulfilled which He spoke, signifying by what death He would die (John 18:28–32 NKJV).

Now as a side note, it's important to understand that the Jews were OK to throw Jesus into the 'defiling' Praetorium building, but they stayed outside so as NOT to defile themselves. It was OK to betray and condemn an innocent man to death, but it was not OK to enter a Roman building. The irony and hypocrisy of their actions are palpable, but the critical point is that the following interaction that Pilate had with Jesus took place away from the ears of the Jews. There may have been guards standing around but what John records next and later were essentially private conversations between Pilate and Jesus. So Jesus was placed in the Praetorium and Pilate went out to the Jews to have the above conversation. He then returns back to Jesus, and we see the full interaction:

> Then Pilate entered the Praetorium again, called Jesus, and said to Him, "Are You the King of the Jews?" Jesus answered him, "Are you speaking for yourself about this, or did others tell you this concerning Me?" Pilate answered, "Am I a Jew? Your own nation and the chief priests have delivered You to me. What have You done?" Jesus answered, "My kingdom is not of this world. If My kingdom were of this world, My servants would fight, so that I should not be delivered to the Jews; but now My kingdom is not from here." Pilate therefore said to Him, "Are You a king then?" Jesus answered, "You say rightly that I am a king. For this cause I was born, and for this cause I have come into the world, that I should bear witness to the truth. Everyone who is of the truth hears My voice." Pilate said to Him, "What is truth?" And when he had said this, he went out again to the Jews, and said to them, "I find no fault in Him at all" (John 18:33–38 NKJV).

So it wasn't exactly a single statement of Jesus declaring Himself the King of the Jews that Pilate responded to when he said: "*I find no fault in Him at all.*" Pilate realized that Jesus was, as far as he could tell, not leading an insurrection and was of no danger to the Roman government. Pilate now takes Jesus out of the Praetorium to face his accusers. This is when Jesus refuses to engage the Jewish leaders and goes totally silent. Mark says it like this:

> And the chief priests accused Him of many things, but He answered nothing. Then Pilate asked Him again, saying, "Do You answer nothing? See how many things they testify against You!" But Jesus still answered nothing, so that Pilate marveled (Mark 15:3–5 NKJV).

An interesting twist comes into the narrative at this point; this one ONLY recorded by Luke. Pilate again declares Christ's innocence, but the response of the Jews opens up a possible exit plan from this sticky situation for Pilate. Let's pick it up in Luke 23:

> So Pilate said to the chief priests and the crowd, "I find no fault in this Man." But they were the more fierce, saying, "He stirs up the people, teaching throughout all Judea, beginning from Galilee to this place." (Luke 23:4–6 NKJV).

Jesus Faces Herod

> When Pilate heard of Galilee, he asked if the Man were a Galilean. And as soon as he knew that He belonged to Herod's jurisdiction, he sent Him to Herod, who was also in Jerusalem at that time. Now when Herod saw Jesus, he was exceedingly glad; for he had desired for a long time to see Him, because he had heard many things about Him, and he hoped to see some miracle done by Him. Then he questioned Him with many words, but He answered him nothing. And the chief priests and scribes stood and vehemently accused Him
> (Luke 23:6–10 NKJV).

It's an interesting study to research who Jesus speaks to and who He doesn't. Probably one of the scariest things that can happen to a human being is when God refuses to engage them or even give them a single word of interaction. Jesus answered the high priest Annas but NOT Caiaphas, at least not until He was put under oath. He spoke to Pilate but NOT to Herod, not even a word. Herod finally gives up but not without giving permission for his soldiers to mistreat Jesus.

> Then Herod, with his men of war, treated Him with contempt and mocked Him, arrayed Him in a gorgeous robe, and sent Him back to Pilate (Luke 23:11 NKJV).

The fate of Jesus is now back on Pilate's plate. Somehow the fact that Pilate even recognized Herod's possible jurisdiction over Jesus caused a previously strained relationship to be reconciled. I think Pilate was not so much as trying to honor Herod but rather trying to avoid having to be responsible for the condemnation of an innocent human being. Here is how Luke describes that reconciliation:

That very day Pilate and Herod became friends with each other, for previously they had been at enmity with each other (Luke 23:12 NKJV).

When most Christians look at the story of Pontius Pilate and what happens next after Jesus returns from Herod, they immediately jump to conclusions concerning him. Probably no other political leader in history has had to make such a tortured decision. It is only when we take a balanced look at all four accounts of this story, do we see the humanity of this man Pilate and why Jesus gave him such significant time and interaction. When you understand some of the specific details that now unfold in the narrative, I believe you will never again see this story in the same light.

Let's continue Luke's telling of the story. Pilate tries again to plead for some sense with the Jewish leaders, and he offers to have Jesus scourged. This is a severe punishment often used to extract a confession from an accused criminal but also used as a terrible infliction of pain as a penalty for a crime. In Pilate's mind, he was hoping to satisfy the Jew's desire for harsh punishment but keep it short of execution. I'm going to use the New Living Translation as it makes this next passage much clearer.

> Then Pilate called together the leading priests and other religious leaders, along with the people, and he announced his verdict. "You brought this man to me, accusing him of leading a revolt. I have examined him thoroughly on this point in your presence and find him innocent. Herod came to the same conclusion and sent him back to us. Nothing this man has done calls for the death penalty. So I will have him flogged, and then I will release him." Then a mighty roar rose from the crowd, and with one voice they shouted, "Kill him." (Luke 23:13–18 NLT).

Jesus Versus Barabbas

Pilate suddenly sees a very feasible way out of this horrible situation that is escalating by the minute. It's a Passover custom that has been in existence for many years, and he brings it up to the crowd. Let's follow Matthew's description:

> Now it was the governor's custom each year during the Passover celebration to release one prisoner to the crowd—anyone they wanted. This year there was a notorious prisoner, a man named Barabbas. As the crowds gathered before Pilate's house that morning, he asked them, "Which one do you want me to release to you—Barabbas, or Jesus who is called the Messiah?" (He knew very well that the religious

leaders had arrested Jesus out of envy.) Just then, as Pilate was sitting on the judgment seat, his wife sent him this message: "Leave that innocent man alone. I suffered through a terrible nightmare about him last night." Meanwhile, the leading priests and the elders persuaded the crowd to ask for Barabbas to be released and for Jesus to be put to death. So the governor asked again, "Which of these two do you want me to release to you?" The crowd shouted back, "Barabbas!" Pilate responded, "Then what should I do with Jesus who is called the Messiah?" They shouted back, "Crucify him!" "Why?" Pilate demanded. "What crime has he committed?" But the mob roared even louder, "Crucify him!" (Matthew 27:15–23 NLT)

Some huge facts emerge in these verses from Matthew. Firstly we see that Pilate correctly perceives the deceit of the Jewish leaders. He understands that envy is behind their wicked actions. He also likely perceived their manipulation of the crowd. To put this situation in a contemporary context, it would be like offering a modern crowd the choice between Mandela and Charles Manson. It would seem nonsensical for the crowd to choose Manson, but the Scriptures in ALL four Gospels tell us the people chose a murderer over Jesus Christ. The behavior of the crowd in Pilate's mind was bizarre, and the easiest pathway out of this horrible situation was suddenly now closed.

And then a message is handed to Pilate from his wife telling him to *"leave that innocent man alone."* The New King James Version says: *"Have nothing to do with that JUST Man, because I have suffered many things today in a dream because of Him."* I cannot even imagine what Pilate must have thought when he got this message. It would shock me if his wife EVER before had tried to interfere in his job or in his judgments over the people. Whatever warning she got, it shows that God allowed her to see some glimpse of the consequences of the decision her husband was about to make. Again, the fact that there was spiritual warning means that God respected Pilate and his wife enough to allow this warning to be delivered.

To fully appreciate what happens next, we need to switch over to John's recording of the next sequences of events. In the other Gospels, the narrative moves quickly to crucifixion, but that is NOT what happened. Pilate is not done fighting. He follows through on his plan now to scourge Jesus and let him go. Let's pick it up in John's Gospel, chapter 19.

Jesus is Flogged

> Then Pilate had Jesus flogged with a lead-tipped whip. The soldiers wove a crown of thorns and put it on his head, and they put a purple robe on him. "Hail! King of the Jews!" they mocked, as they slapped him across the face (John 19:1–3 NLT).

Those who saw the movie *The Passion of the Christ* will never forget the sheer brutality of that flogging scene. The soldiers not only whipped Jesus mercilessly, almost to the point of death, but they also twisted a crown of thorns and put it on his head. From the Old Testament prophecies, we can surmise that they also ripped portions of his beard from his face. Isaiah prophecies the following about this flogging:

> I gave My back to those who struck Me, And My cheeks to those who plucked out the beard; I did not hide My face from shame and spitting. "For the LORD God will help Me; Therefore I will not be disgraced; Therefore I have set My face like a flint, And I know that I will not be ashamed" (Isaiah 50:6–7 NKJV).

We also know from Isaiah that the stripes across the back of Jesus secured healing from sickness and disease for every believing Christian:

> Surely He has borne our griefs and carried our sorrows; Yet we esteemed Him stricken, Smitten by God, and afflicted. But He was wounded for our transgressions, He was bruised for our iniquities; The chastisement for our peace was upon Him, And by His stripes we are healed (Isaiah 53:4–5 NKJV).

Pilate was hoping that the horror of this brutal flogging by the Roman soldiers would be enough to satisfy the crowd. The soldiers I'm sure at this point were demonically inspired. They went further than any normal criminal situation warranted in inflicting severe damage on the physical body of Christ. They then thrust the crown of thorns on his head and put a purple robe on him. From John's account, Pilate at this stage had NOT yet given the crucifixion order. This is critical, so you understand what happens next. Let's continue from the New King James Version in John 19 where we see that Pilate still believes his brutal treatment of Christ would surely be enough punishment to satisfy the seething crowd:

> Pilate then went out again, and said to them, "Behold, I am bringing Him out to you, that you may know that I find no fault in Him." Then Jesus came out, wearing the crown of thorns and the purple robe. And Pilate said to them, "Behold the Man!" Therefore, when the chief priests and officers saw Him, they cried out, saying, "Crucify Him, crucify Him!" Pilate said to them, "You take Him and crucify Him, for I find no fault in Him." The Jews answered him, "We have a law, and according to our law He ought to die, because He made Himself the Son of God." Therefore, when Pilate heard that saying, he was the more afraid (John 19:4–5 NKJV).

The original accusation that Jesus had called Himself **the King of the Jews** was only a mask to politically manipulate Pilate. By casting the accusation against Jesus in political terms, they had hoped to get an easy judgment. Pilate was no fool. He knew the Jewish leaders had no respect for Caesar. That's why their original arguments never moved Pilate and why he repeatedly declared Jesus innocent in front of the crowd. I think Pilate assumed Jesus had violated some religious law and that he could sufficiently punish Him to satisfy the crowd. When the leaders saw that this political tack was not going to get them an execution, they finally revealed their hand. Pilate knew there was jealousy, but he did not know the original accusation from the house of Caiaphas upon which the Jews had based their decision to extract a death penalty.

Pilate in this John 19:6 Scripture was even willing to turn Jesus over to the Sanhedrin and turn a blind eye if they executed Him. He actually says to them, *"You take Him and crucify Him, for I find no fault in Him."* Like modern day politicians, the Jewish leaders first used a politically correct justification to push their case (threatening Caesar's kingship), but their motivations were completely driven by the claim of Jesus to be the Son of God and the Messiah. Suddenly Pilate understood the whole situation, and it terrified him. He pulls Jesus back into the Praetorium for a final one-on-one conversation with the Son of God.

> Therefore, when Pilate heard that saying, he was the more afraid, and went again into the Praetorium, and said to Jesus, "Where are You from?" But Jesus gave him no answer. Then Pilate said to Him, "Are You not speaking to me? Do You not know that I have power to crucify You, and power to release You?" Jesus answered, "You could have no power at all against Me unless it had been given you from above. Therefore the one who delivered Me to you has the greater sin." From then on Pilate sought to release Him (John 19:8–12 NKJV).

After reading everything in the four Gospels, I truly believe that Pilate, up until this point, had tried every normal technique he knew to release Jesus. Until this final interaction with Jesus, Pilate thought he was in control of the situation. He had tried pushing the judgment of Jesus over to Herod, and he tried scourging Him to extract any misconduct and satisfy the crowd, he tried giving the crowd the absurd option of Barabbas versus Jesus, and he tried declaring the innocence of Jesus before the Jewish leaders and the crowd on numerous occasions. He had marveled at how Jesus had conducted Himself in front of His accusers, and he had received a frantic but clear warning not to touch this prisoner from his wife who likely never involved herself in his affairs. Nothing about this situation was normal.

Probably most disturbing to Pilate's soul were the one-on-one encounters he had with the Son of God. To Pilate's credit, Jesus at least spoke to him whereas He had refused to speak a single word to Herod. I think that Pilate suddenly had the revelation that the One who stood before him was no ordinary man. Something changed at this late juncture in Pilate's disposition. The Gospel of John simply says: ***"From then on Pilate sought to release Him."*** This became a personal crusade for Pilate, and he was going to give it his best shot. It surely appears he was trying to get Jesus released before this point, but now it became a desperate, all-out effort.

It is also at this point that the screws begin to tighten on Pilate to force him to crucify Jesus. Talk about wicked people throwing the political playbook at Pilate. The religious leaders and the crowd now threaten to destroy Pilate's political career over this one decision. The Jewish leaders pivot back to Pilate's most vulnerable weakness, his need to demonstrate unquestionable loyalty to Rome and to Caesar. They are going to use that political tack whether it violates truth or not.

Pilate knew he had used up all his options. The crowd was not open to reason, they had chosen a murderer over a righteous Man, they were threatening to destroy his political future, and they were about to riot and get ugly as a crowd. The brutal scourging of Jesus had not appeased them and the Jewish leaders, driven by pure jealousy and hatred for Jesus, are stirring the people to a point where only the death penalty and a bloody crucifixion will satiate the crowd.

It's extremely interesting to read the specific language that Pilate uses from here forward with the crowd and with the religious leaders. Something deep in Pilate's perception had happened through his interactions with Jesus. I truly believe that somehow Pilate at this point had come to believe that Jesus was who He said He was, the eternal King of the Jews. Pilate now brings Jesus back out to the crowd, and this is where we need to note his specific language.

> From then on Pilate sought to release Him, but the Jews cried out, saying, "If you let this Man go, you are not Caesar's friend. Whoever makes himself a king speaks against Caesar." When Pilate therefore heard that saying, he brought Jesus out and sat down in the judgment seat in a place that is called The Pavement, but in Hebrew, Gabbatha. Now it was the Preparation Day of the Passover, and about the sixth hour. And he said to the Jews, **"Behold your King!"** But they cried out, "Away with Him, away with Him! Crucify Him!" Pilate said to them, **"Shall I crucify your King?"** The chief priests answered, "We have no king but Caesar!" (John 19:8–15 NKJV)

Only understanding this full picture does the manner of Pilate's judgment, his choice of words and his actions make sense. Pilate comes across as being disgusted with the Jewish leadership and with the manipulated crowd. Matthew takes the narrative to its horrible end.

> Pilate said to them, "What then shall I do with Jesus who is called Christ?" They all said to him, "Let Him be crucified!" Then the governor said, "Why, what evil has He done?" But they cried out all the more, saying, "Let Him be crucified!" When Pilate saw that he could not prevail at all, but rather that a tumult was rising, he took water and washed his hands before the multitude, saying, "I am innocent of the blood of this JUST Person. You see to it." And all the people answered and said, "His blood be on us and on our children."
> (Matthew 27:22–25 NKJV).

This was Pilate's final exchange with the crowd. Pilate takes water and symbolically washes his hands in front of the crowd. He says the words *"I am innocent of the blood of this JUST Person."* With this act of hand washing and use of choice words, Pilate is doing everything he can to declare himself innocent of Christ's blood. Pilate then forces the Jews to say the most damaging thing EVER, and they put the curse of the blood of Jesus Christ, the Messiah on their own heads and on the heads of FUTURE GENERATIONS.

When I worked for Reinhard Bonnke, we did a massive Europe-wide conference event in Birmingham, England. I was the television producer in charge of all media, duplication, translation, and sales. My budget was in the hundreds of thousands of dollars. Of all the messages preached over the four days of that conference, one still stands out 30 years later. It was preached by Reinhard, and it was called "The Blessing and the Curse of the Blood of Jesus." Reinhard shared how many millions in Africa, and other parts of the world have benefited from the blessings released by the blood of Jesus. He obviously was referring to how many millions in his crowds have had their sins forgiven and their illnesses healed.

Reinhard then spoke about the curse of the blood of Jesus on those who reject the Messiah. Reinhard in this message spoke about all the persecution, suffering and tragedy that had happened over the past 2,000 years to the Jewish people. Being from Germany, it was especially poignant when Reinhard spoke about the Holocaust and how some of the consequences reaped by the Jewish nation went back to this one statement of the crowd at the crucifixion of Jesus: *"His blood be on us and on our children."* In the end, these words proved to be tragic but Pilate made sure that before he turned Jesus over for crucifixion, that he had obtained this very specific confession. It is almost unthinkable what happened next:

> [. . .] he (Pilate) delivered Him to be crucified. Then the soldiers of the governor took Jesus into the Praetorium and gathered the whole garrison around Him. And they stripped Him and put a scarlet robe on Him. When they had twisted a crown of thorns, they put it on His head, and a reed in His right hand. And they bowed the knee before Him and mocked Him, saying, "Hail, King of the Jews!" Then they spat on Him, and took the reed and struck Him on the head. And when they had mocked Him, they took the robe off Him, put His own clothes on Him, and led Him away to be crucified
> (Matthew 27:22–31 NKJV).

It's hard to believe that after Jesus had been scourged, and before He was crucified, that He went through one last mocking and beating from the entire garrison of Roman soldiers. This is recorded in both Matthew and Mark. Scholars disagree on exactly how many soldiers were in a garrison, but some say as many as 600. How Jesus endured this final assault by a whole garrison is almost impossible to imagine. The crown of thorns and robe may be a conflagration in the narration of what already had taken place. The assault by the whole garrison appears to be something that happened after the scourging, after the final interaction with Pilate, after the crucifixion decision and right before they led him to Golgotha. Because of the loss of blood, no sleep and the repeated brutal attacks on His physical body, it's no wonder the Roman soldiers had to force Simon of Cyrene to help carry the cross of Christ (Matthew 27:32 NKJV).

This crucifixion decision was a tortured decision for Pilate, one that went against every instinct in his being. Only the threat that his political career and future would be destroyed forced his hand, but not before he had extracted an open confession of personal culpability and blame from the Jewish crowd. In the end, Pilate openly and unashamedly declared that Jesus was the JUST King of the Jews.

Pilate wrote the following as the accusation against Jesus. The accusation was written in Greek, Hebrew, and Latin. The full inscription was **"This is Jesus of Nazareth, the King of the Jews."** Matthew says, *"This is Jesus the King of the Jews."* Mark says, *"The King of the Jews,"* Luke says, *"This is the King of the Jews"* and John says, *"Jesus of Nazareth, the King of the Jews."* The full inscription is a composite of all four. The Jewish leaders tried to get Pilate to change what he had written, but he refused and simply said, *"What I have written, I have written."* I think it's safe to say that Pilate likely believed that what he had written was the truth.

Some may interpret these positions I have outlined from the New Testament as being Jew bashing. Nothing could be further from the truth. My grandfather was 100% Jewish, my daughter has married into a wonderful Jewish family, and each year I lead a team of people to visit the Holy Land. I do NOT believe in replacement theology but believe God's end-time purposes revolve specifically around the Jewish people and their FULL restoration. I even have produced a documentary titled *Thank God For Israel*, outlining four key steps the global Body of Christ can take to support and help Israel in a practical way. These four steps include going to the Holy Land, giving donations to worthy organizations working in Israel, investing financially in Jewish business partnerships, and praying daily for the nation and its people. This horrific rejection of the Messiah by the Jewish people recorded in the New Testament is, I believe, a part of provoking them to reexamine their beliefs about Jesus and His claims to be the Messiah Israel is still waiting for.

The Apostle Peter did not shy away from confronting the Jews of his generation with the way they acted in front of Pilate. In fact, one might think that this was the end of the Pilate story, but it is not. This series of events was the key catalyst that God used in birthing 5,000 people into the New Testament Church early in the book of Acts. We pick the story up in Acts 3.

> Now Peter and John went up together to the temple at the hour of prayer, the ninth hour. And a certain man lame from his mother's womb was carried, whom they laid daily at the gate of the temple which is called Beautiful, to ask alms from those who entered the

> temple; who, seeing Peter and John about to go into the temple, asked for alms. And fixing his eyes on him, with John, Peter said, "Look at us." So he gave them his attention, expecting to receive something from them. Then Peter said, "Silver and gold I do not have, but what I do have I give you: In the name of Jesus Christ of Nazareth, rise up and walk." And he took him by the right hand and lifted him up, and immediately his feet and ankle bones received strength. So he, leaping up, stood and walked and entered the temple with them—walking, leaping, and praising God. And all the people saw him walking and praising God. Then they knew that it was he who sat begging alms at the Beautiful Gate of the temple; and they were filled with wonder and amazement at what had happened to him. Now as the lame man who was healed held on to Peter and John, all the people ran together to them in the porch which is called Solomon's, greatly amazed (Acts 3:1–11 NKJV).

So when Peter saw this miracle, he recognized the opportunity to evangelize the Jewish people. Hundreds and possibly thousands of these same people less than two months before had been in that angry mob with Pilate shouting *"crucify Him."*
Let's look exactly how Peter used the Pilate event to bring in possibly the greatest single harvest of souls recorded in the Book of Acts.

> So when Peter saw it, he responded to the people: "Men of Israel, why do you marvel at this? Or why look so intently at us, as though by our own power or godliness we had made this man walk? **The God of Abraham, Isaac, and Jacob, the God of our fathers, glorified His Servant Jesus, whom:**
>
> **YOU delivered up and denied in the presence of Pilate when he was determined to let Him go.**
>
> **But YOU denied the Holy One and the Just, and asked for a murderer to be granted to you, and**
>
> **(YOU) killed the Prince of life, whom God raised from the dead, of which we are witnesses.**
>
> **And His name, through faith in His name, has made this man strong, whom you see and know.** Yes, the faith which comes through

> Him has given him this perfect soundness in the presence of you all, "Yet now, brethren, I know that you did it in ignorance, as did also your rulers. But those things which God foretold by the mouth of all His prophets, that the Christ would suffer, He has thus fulfilled. **Repent therefore and be converted, that your sins may be blotted out, so that times of refreshing may come from the presence of the Lord, and that He may send Jesus Christ**, who was preached to you before, whom heaven must receive until the times of restoration of all things, which God has spoken by the mouth of all His holy prophets since the world began (Acts 3:12–26 NKJV).

Luke writes in Acts 4:4 that about 5,000 men responded to this message and that did not include the women and the children. We see clearly here that Peter specifically mentions that the same Jewish people as were alive less than two months after the crucifixion chose a murderer over Jesus and that they were responsible for *"killing the Prince of life"* and that they had denied Jesus in the presence of Pilate when Pilate was *"determined to let Him go."* This tough preaching caused a deep repentance and thousands were swept into the Kingdom of the Messiah.

In breaking down this interaction between Pilate, Jesus, and the Jewish people, we see the value of exploring the depths, sequencing, perspectives, and nuances in the biblical narrative. What results is a mature, balanced understanding of the story, a deeper appreciation and understanding of the character of Pilate and the extraordinary complexity of the forces at play when he made one of history's gravest and most pivotal decisions.

CHAPTER TWELVE
Maturity and Balance

*The king (Nebuchadnezzar) talked with them, and no one impressed him as much as Daniel, Hananiah, Mishael, and Azariah. So they entered the royal service. Whenever the king consulted them in any matter requiring wisdom and **balanced** judgment, he found them ten times more capable than any of the magicians and enchanters in his entire kingdom*

— Daniel 1:19–20 NLT

*O God, I beg two favors from you; let me have them before I die. First, help me never to tell a lie. Second, give me neither poverty nor riches! Give me just enough to satisfy my needs. For if I grow rich, I may deny you and say, "Who is the L*ORD*?" And if I am too poor, I may steal and thus insult God's holy name*

— Proverbs 30:7 NLT

Many years ago I was speaking with a wonderful minister of God from South Africa by the name of Alan Platt. Alan heads up a network of churches by the name of Doxa Deo, and he is a profound thinker and preacher. Now I never heard his message about balance, but I simply heard him share in a few sentences the concept behind a message he had recently preached. The concept was that everything in the universe that God created is in a dynamic tension and balance. In fact, what he specifically said was that nearly all TRUTH could be found in a tension between two seemingly contradictory and opposing factors.

For example, on one side of Scripture you have God's incredible and amazing grace but on the other side of Scripture is God's Law and His judgment. Somewhere in the middle is a place for a Christian believer to walk where they are not in one ditch or the other. They are balanced right in the middle trusting in God's grace but also fearing the consequences of God's judgment if they were to go astray. Another way to look at this is to understand that Jesus is the Lion of the Tribe of Judah but also the Lamb of God who takes away the sins of the world. We have to know Him in both dimensions of His character and nature. They may seem contradictory, but maturity is finding the perfect middle ground.

I was so intrigued by this concept that I began to really think it through. As a golf player, I greatly prefer to hit the golf ball down the middle of the fairway and do not like to stray either side into the rough or into whatever hazards lie off the nice green grass that provides the easiest shots to the green. Jesus talked about people leading others into a ditch, and we know when driving, staying in the center of your lane is the safest place to travel.

So I really began to consider these dynamic tensions that we face in life and throughout Scripture. Let's look more closely at this one:

> "Therefore consider the **goodness and severity** of God."
> (Romans 11:22 NKJV).

To truly understand God, you need to know both His goodness and His severity. One of the greatest figures in the Bible was Moses. Moses saw amazing miracles, from the burning bush to the plagues in Egypt to the parting of the Red Sea. He also saw all of God's goodness pass before him as we see in this interaction between Moses and God.

> And he (Moses) said, "Please, show me Your glory." Then He (God) said, "I will make all My **goodness** pass before you, and I will proclaim the name of the LORD before you. I will be gracious to whom I will be gracious, and I will have compassion on whom I will have compassion" (Exodus 33:18 NKJV).

> Now the LORD descended in the cloud and stood with him there, and proclaimed the name of the LORD. And the LORD passed before him and proclaimed, "The LORD, the LORD God, merciful and gracious, long suffering, and abounding in goodness and truth, keeping mercy for thousands, forgiving iniquity and transgression and sin, by no means clearing the guilty, visiting the iniquity of the fathers upon the children and the children's children to the third and the fourth generation" (Exodus 34:5-7 NKJV).

We see in the Torah (first five books of the Old Testament) the children of Israel commit some terrible misdeeds before God, especially when they worshipped a golden calf after the HUGE miracles in Egypt and the Red Sea crossing. The Bible says that Moses stood in the gap at that time and, because of Moses, God did NOT destroy Israel. When it says that Moses stood in the gap, we are NOT talking about some token prayer. We are talking about two 40-day fasts back to back with NO BREAD and NO WATER. Here is how Moses describes these in the book of Deuteronomy as he is speaking to the children of Israel and reminding them of their sin:

> Remember! Do not forget how you provoked the Lord your God to wrath in the wilderness. From the day that you departed from the land of Egypt until you came to this place, you have been rebellious against the Lord. Also in Horeb you provoked the Lord to wrath, so that the Lord was angry enough with you to have destroyed you. When I went up into the mountain to receive the tablets of stone, the tablets of the covenant which the Lord made with you, then I stayed on the mountain forty days and forty nights. **I neither ate bread nor drank water**. Then the Lord delivered to me two tablets of stone written with the finger of God, and on them were all the words which the Lord had spoken to you on the mountain from the midst of the fire in the day of the assembly. And it came to pass, at the **end of forty days and forty nights, that the Lord gave me the two tablets of stone**, the tablets of the covenant. Then the Lord said to me, "Arise, go down quickly from here, for your people whom you brought out of Egypt have acted corruptly; they have quickly turned aside from the way which I commanded them; they have made themselves a molded image." Furthermore the Lord spoke to me, saying, "I have seen this people, and indeed they are a stiff-necked people. Let Me alone, that I may destroy them and blot out their name from under heaven; and I will make of you a nation mightier and greater than they." So I turned and came down from the mountain, and the mountain burned with fire; and the two tablets of the covenant were in my two hands. And I looked, and behold, you had sinned against the Lord your God—had made for yourselves a molded calf! You had turned aside quickly from the way which the Lord had commanded you. Then I took the two tablets and threw them out of my two hands and broke them before your eyes. **And I fell down before the Lord, as at the first, forty days and forty nights; I neither ate bread nor drank water**, because of all your sin which you committed in doing wickedly in the sight of the Lord, to provoke Him to anger. For I was afraid of the anger and hot displeasure with which the Lord was angry with you, to destroy you. But the Lord listened to me at that time also
> (Deuteronomy 9:7–19 NKJV).

If you examine chapters 9 and 10 of Deuteronomy, you will find that Moses did FOUR 40-day fasts and kept prostrating himself until God's anger relented and He spared the people of Israel. Here is how Moses described another such fast when the children of Israel refused to go in to possess the land:

> "Thus I prostrated myself before the LORD; forty days and forty nights I kept **prostrating** myself, because the LORD had said He would destroy you" (Deuteronomy 9:25 NKJV).

Just a few verses later, in Chapter 10:10 we see Moses referring to a fourth 40-day fast:

> "As at the first time, I stayed in the mountain forty days and forty nights; the LORD also heard me at that time, and the LORD chose not to destroy you. Then the LORD said to me, 'Arise, begin your journey before the people, that they may go in and possess the land which I swore to their fathers to give them'" (Deuteronomy 10:10 NKJV).

If anyone knew God, it was Moses. He only left us ONE psalm, and that is Psalms 90. Here are some choice verses out of that Psalm that is only 17 verses long:

> 7 For we have been consumed by Your anger, and by Your wrath we are terrified.
>
> 9 For all our days have passed away in Your wrath;
>
> 11 Who knows the power of Your anger? For as the fear of You, so is Your wrath.

It's sobering to realize that the person who knew God best in the Old Testament not only understood His goodness but also profoundly understood God's anger and wrath. He knew both the GOODNESS and SEVERITY of God and lived in a BALANCED understanding of those two aspects of God's character.

Other Tensions in Life and Scripture

How about the tension between God's Word and His Spirit? A well-known minister in the United States said the following: "If you have all Word and NO Spirit, you will dry up. If you have all Spirit and NO Word, you will blow up, but if you have both the Spirit and the Word, you will grow up." That is an apt quote for a book about *growing up* to maturity.

The best churches I know are places of balance. These are places where the GIFTS of the Holy Spirit and the FRUIT of the Holy Spirit are equally taught and exercised. They are places where there is a balance between the spiritual needs of people and the natural needs of people. It's not one or the other, and it's a balance between both. As

CHAPTER 12: MATURITY AND BALANCE

my high school motto (Hilton College) in South Africa reads, "*Orando et Laborando*" which means "By Prayer AND Work."

As mature believers, we need to have balanced relationships, a balanced diet, a balanced checkbook and a balanced approach to Scripture. On a lighter note, we can notice that Jesus fed the multitudes both bread and fish, providing a balance between proteins and carbohydrates and in 1 Kings, we find how Elijah was fed by the birds. *"The ravens brought him bread and meat in the morning, and bread and meat in the evening; and he drank from the brook"* (1 Kings 17:6 NKJV).

Sometimes it can be confusing, and there are times when it feels like we, as Christian believers, are getting mixed messages. When it comes to giving, you have to balance between messages that we as Christians need to sell everything and give it to the poor, not sow sparingly, be a generous hilarious giver, step on faith's waters, trust God for more on one side AND be a responsible steward, be wise, don't live beyond your means, don't carry debt, have a retirement, have a savings, put money away, leave an inheritance for your children and grandchildren on the other side. How do you BALANCE those two opposite sides of a dynamic tension?

Galatians chapter 6 seems to have two contradictory instructions by the Apostle Paul to God's people just three verses apart. In verse 2 he tells believers to *"bear one another's burdens,"* but in verse 5 he says *"for each one shall bear his own load."* Well, which one is it? It's actually a dynamic tension between the two. Everyone needs to do their best to take responsibility for themselves, but when they cannot make it, then others need to help. Both can be true at the same time.

When it comes to pastoral care, there is an equal responsibility on the part of the pastor and leaders on one side and the individual congregation members on the other. The Scriptures tell leaders they will give an account for their flock, that they are responsible to feed them God's Word, and that they will one day present their members as a chaste virgin to Christ (2 Corinthians 11:2). On the part of the members, there is the parable of the ten virgins in Matthew 25 where each virgin is responsible for getting oil for their lamp and in Revelation 19:7 it says that the bride has made herself ready. Both leaders and members have to work in a dynamic relationship and meet in the middle in order for discipleship to really work.

I especially feel this tension as an employer of over 30 people in two for-profit preschools my wife and I manage. How do you be compassionate and caring for your employees, provide benefits and high salaries for them, and still generate a profit while on the other side charging affordable prices for people's high-quality childcare. Sometimes it feels like a high wire balancing act.

Leaders in all spheres of business and ministry are referees calling the shots in a game where they often don't fully understand the dynamics or the rules. So many of our everyday decisions were never taught to us in business school or in a Bible school. Just take human resources, the great minefield. There are so many unwritten rules. If you let someone go, you have to bear the thoughts of how your actions might impact people's families, the morale of the other employees, the children of those families, the friends, and your reputation among your clients and vendors. You also can be accused of a seemingly endless list of "isms." Poor performance by the employee is no longer an antidote to anything. Sometimes it can be so daunting you seriously end up thinking twice about hiring again, and I am one who has a whole chapter on the blessings and benefits of employment. Again it is a dynamic tension.

In the natural, we can only walk if the balance in our inner ears is working. The system in our inner ear that coordinates balance is called the vestibular system. I like the way the website **vestibular.org** describes balance:

> "Balance is the ability to maintain the body's center of mass over its base of support. A properly functioning balance system allows humans to see clearly while moving, identify orientation with respect to gravity, determine direction and speed of movement, and make automatic postural adjustments to maintain posture and stability in various conditions and activities.
>
> Balance is achieved and maintained by a complex set of sensorimotor control systems that include sensory input from vision (sight), proprioception (touch), and the vestibular system (motion, equilibrium, spatial orientation); integration of that sensory input; and motor output to the eye and body muscles. Injury, disease, certain drugs, or the aging process can affect one or more of these components. In addition to the contribution of sensory information, there may also be psychological factors that impair our sense of balance."

We often take balance for granted, but when people have extreme vertigo or lose their sense of balance, it is a serious problem.

If you look at the way God designed the whole universe, everything is in balance. The planets are in a dynamic orbit in their movement around the sun. From the macro to the micro, everything is in dynamic tension. Protons, neutrons, and electrons spin around each other in a sophisticated, balanced way. All of nature is in this tension, and we frequently talk about the "balance of nature" because every ecosystem on the planet has intricate balances between light, water, soil, plants and every creature that lives in that environment.

Jordan Peterson – Chaos and Order
Jordan Peterson, who I mentioned earlier in Chapter 2, believes the correct balance in life is between order and chaos. He has a whole new book titled *12 Rules for Life: An Antidote to Chaos*. He sees order and chaos as being the two ditches every person has to navigate between. That tension, he contends, is also between the right side of the brain and the left: the one side being the rational side and the other being the creative and imaginative side. It's the Yin and the Yang of Chinese philosophy. This dynamic tension can also be found in the differences between male and female. These are just a few facets of this tension and divide.

In addition, Peterson describes chaos as being the unknown, the unexpected, the tragedy of losing a loved one, hopelessness, the horror of darkness, when fear grips, the betrayal of a spouse, the monster under the bed, when life seems to have no meaning and the snake that eternally lurks in the garden. Chaos is also the excitement of boldly going where no one else has gone. It is the side that pushes people to the edge of the metaphysical and also is the place of mystery, creativity, prophetic insight, spirituality, dreams, visions and adventure.

Order, on the other hand, is when everything is working properly when the trains run on time when you have a happy and secure home. Order keeps the operating room clean at the hospital. Order is an island of stability in a sea of ignorance. Order is what God called out of chaos at the beginning of time. It's the walls of the city, the principles of the constitution and the uniform of the policeman. When taken to an extreme, it becomes rigid and tyrannical and produces entities like the Soviet Union and Nazi Germany.

According to Peterson, the quality of our 'being' as individual people is how we manage the balance between these two extremes of ORDER and CHAOS. Here is how he described it in a TEDx Talk® delivered in 2011 in Toronto, Canada:

"When chaos and order are balanced, we have one foot in each domain. That's the meaning that life more abundantly depends on. In that place, we're secure and confident but challenged enough to be alert and developing. In that place we play each game, not just to win, but to become better players at all games in the future. Such meaning properly nurtured can produce a love for life and gratitude so deep that the terrible limitations of 'being' are justified. It is in this manner that Paradise is regained.

The alternative is to live an unbalanced life. This is not good because the terrible forces of chaos and order will tear an unbalanced person apart. He will become overwhelmed, hopeless, bitter, vengeful, and finally, cruel. She will become willfully blind, narrow, bored, cynical, and vicious. When life is unbalanced, people work against it because they're angry at the dreadful limited conditions of existence. "To hell with it." That's the curse of the embittered. Hell is where they're headed and where they'd like to drag everyone else."

Peterson believes that every human being needs BOTH order and chaos in their lives. Too much order produces a dry, predictable and boring person. Too much chaos sends people into instability, fear, and weirdness. In the political realm, he says, we need both the Republicans and the Democrats or the liberals and the conservatives. He says societies will always create hierarchies, and those will create winners and losers. The tendency when people at the top, from either side of the spectrum, get too much power and money is that they, all too often, become corrupt and tyrannical. If that happens, it will create a lot of disenfranchised people at the bottom of the hierarchy, and that is why you need an opposition party to represent the poor, downtrodden and disenfranchised of society. A healthy opposition will cause either a peaceful change in government through the democratic process or anarchy and government overthrow. Where a tyrannical leader or dictator arises, like what happened in the former Soviet Union or in Hitler's Germany, and there is no opposition allowed, then millions are likely to die through tyranny and unrestrained power. Balance, therefore, is essential in all spheres of life.

The Apostle Paul in Ephesians chapter 4 talks about Christians coming to a place of maturity where they are stable, where they walk with wisdom and stability. He says we should reach this place where:

CHAPTER 12: MATURITY AND BALANCE

> [. . .] we should no longer be children, tossed to and fro and carried about with every wind of doctrine, by the trickery of men, in the cunning craftiness of deceitful plotting, but, speaking the truth in love, may grow up in all things into Him who is the head – Christ – from whom the whole body, joined and knit together by what every joint supplies, according to the effective working by which every part does its share, causes growth of the body for the edifying of itself in love (Ephesians 4:14–16 NKJV).

In other words, we are not only to be balanced within ourselves and in our grasp of doctrine but also be balanced in our relationships to each other. We are a balanced body where every person relates to each other in a balanced, proper and orderly way.

This type of personal and corporate balance also requires that each believer knows exactly which part of Christ's body they are created to be. Many years ago, while doing my Masters degree in television production at Regent University in Virginia Beach, I attended the First Assembly of God Church led at that time by Pastor Wally Odum. Over thirty years later, I still remember, in detail, many of his sermons and illustrations. For example one Mother's Day message he started by reading the first six verses of the Gospel of Matthew. For those familiar with these verses, it's a very cumbersome genealogy about people begetting people. It seemed like a very strange foundational Scripture for a Mother's Day message.

After Wally had read this complicated genealogy, he pointed out that the begetting included the names of FOUR mothers who were Tamar, Rahab, Ruth, and Bathsheba. What followed was a brilliant Mother's day message as Wally unpacked the lives of these four incredible mothers and brought out that it was NO accident that their names appeared in the FIRST SIX versus of the New Testament.

What made the services I attended at First Assembly of God so powerful was the way their worship leader led everyone into God's presence. At just the right time, he would pass the baton over to Wally, and the Word of God would come forth like fire. I loved the dynamic of those services and always left feeling so fed and fulfilled EXCEPT for ONE time. Wally had traveled that weekend but, not to worry, he left that magnificent worship leader in charge of the message that week. Well, that worship leader turned his worship job over to someone else so he could focus on preaching the sermon for the week. It was a total disaster. The worship did not even slightly hit the mark, and the message was absolutely horrible. As I left that service, I remember understanding, in a very clear way, how people who are fantastic in one place in the Body of Christ, can be a disaster when they are in the wrong place.

Years later, in 1991, I ministered at Abbott Loop Community Church in Alaska. Their model of church planting in teams later became the prototype for the ISOM program. Over an 18-year period, they sent out about 1,300 of their church members in teams to plant new churches, and they were very mature at developing biblical eldership. Two five-part courses from Abbott Loop leaders ended up being included in the ISOM program, the first was Jim Feeney's *The Team Method of Church Planting* and then the Apostle of that church, Dick Benjamin, gave us five hours on *Biblical Eldership*. I think that Abbott Loop is one of the only churches I have ever been to where the pastor preached his message and then turned it over to the evangelist to do the altar call and where they had ordained prophets who had access to a microphone during the service to give prophetic words to the congregation. Each of the five-fold ministries was proven in character and gifting and then ordained into a specific function within the life of the church. Today they may not function in that way, but in that season of maturity, they certainly did.

When Christ's Body is in balance, and when each part of the Body of Christ knows its function and place, then tremendous growth and blessing will result. Believers need to understand who they ARE and, just as importantly, who they ARE NOT. Paul says we need ALL of the fivefold ministry gifts inputting into our lives IN BALANCE to grow to maturity. Think of this concept as you once again read Ephesians 4:11-14 NKJV:

> Now these are the gifts Christ gave to the church: the apostles, the prophets, the evangelists, and the pastors and teachers. Their responsibility is to equip God's people to do his work and build up the church, the body of Christ. This will continue until we all come to such unity in our faith and knowledge of God's Son that we will be **mature in the LORD**, measuring up to the full and complete standard of Christ. Then we will **no longer be immature** like children. We won't be tossed and blown about by every wind of new teaching [...]

Somehow, we need ALL of the fivefold ministries IN BALANCE to bring us personally and corporately to maturity.

Back to my friend Alan Platt from South Africa. He only shared with me the concept of truth often being found in a dynamic tension between two seemingly contradictory sides. He then, at a different time, shared with me a second concept without again telling me almost any details. He said it was NOT ONLY the Old Testament that had laws like the 10 Commandments, and the New Testament had them too. That took me on a new and profound journey of discovery.

CHAPTER THIRTEEN

New Testament Laws

"Laws control the lesser man. Right conduct controls the greater one."

— *Chinese Proverb*

The New Testament LAWS are, in many ways, more difficult to keep than the Old Testament laws. You see, back in the Old Testament, the rules were very black and white. If you violated any law, there was a procedure of judgment, penalty, and atonement. The New Testament laws are different and much more nuanced. They require a greater sensitivity to the Holy Spirit and to fellow believers. Although many pastors refuse to teach this, we still have laws under the New Testament, but they look VERY different from those in the Old Testament. They require a lot more maturity to understand and to KEEP. If a person has NOT learned to grasp these and walk in them, they are still babes in Christ. Here are some of those HIGHER New Testament laws:

1) Higher Law 1 — The Law of the Spirit of Life in Christ Jesus

> *"You will become as small as your controlling desire;*
> *as great as your dominant aspiration."*

— James Allen

Paul speaks about this LAW in Romans 8:

> *There is* therefore now no condemnation to those who are in Christ Jesus, who do not walk according to the flesh, but according to the Spirit. For the **law of the Spirit of life in Christ Jesus** has made me free from the **law of sin and death** (Romans 8:1-2 NKJV).

Paul is talking here about a law in the New Testament that will dominate and overcome the Old Testament system of legal penalty, which he refers to as the **law of sin and death**. Understanding this concept is incredibly important.

In my first book, I had a whole chapter called "Conquering the Sin Nature." The core understanding of that chapter and an accompanying teaching in the ISOM is that the existence of the sin nature is NOT sin to God because we all have it from Adam. Paul twice in Romans 7 says that *"Now if I do what I will not to do, it is no longer I who do it, but sin that dwells in me"* (Romans 7:20 NKJV).

Paul understood that the sin nature in him WAS NOT HIM. There was NO CONDEMNATION because he understood that his sin nature in God's eyes was DEAD. I made this statement in that teaching that "the existence of the sin nature is NOT sin to God but yielding to the sin nature IS sin to God."

Most people have NO victory in conquering the sin nature because they try and fight the flesh with their will and with their good intentions. They try and fight the flesh using the Old Testament **law of sin and death**. Fighting the flesh with the flesh like people did in the Old Testament is futile. Only when a person understands that there is a higher law, which is the law of the Spirit of life in Christ Jesus, will they be able to start walking in victory. This is where a believer learns to understand that their flesh nature is NOT THEM but is DEAD in God's eyes. That understanding alone will begin to set them free from the law of sin and death. That is why Paul says to the Romans: *"Likewise you also, **reckon** yourselves to be dead indeed to sin, but alive to God in Christ Jesus our LORD"* (Romans 6:11 NKJV).

The key here is THINKING of your flesh nature as being DEAD and intentionally considering it NOT being you. That is what it means to RECKON. The devil's greatest lie to Christians is to convince them that their flesh nature IS them. While a Christian believes that lie, they will NEVER have victory. They MUST believe in the **law of the Spirit of Life in Christ Jesus**. That is why Paul says: *"For if you live according to the flesh you will die; but if by the Spirit you put to death the deeds of the body, you will live"* (Romans 8:13 NKJV).

So the key to victory is to think of your flesh nature as being dead and NOT YOU and learning to apply this law of allowing the Holy Spirit to conquer the flesh nature in your life by yielding to His power. Learning to put this law into action has probably been the single greatest revelation in my life that has helped me build the global ministry that I have today. With all the good teaching I had as a young Christian, I NEVER had someone explain this properly to me. Because of that, I struggled needlessly for 13 years trying to get the victory by my own strength and believing the lie that my fleshly thoughts and desires were the real ME.

As soon as I understood that the real ME in God's eyes was the born-again person who wanted to serve God despite my flesh nature, I began the long journey to NOT having condemnation. I began learning to yield to the Holy Spirit and to allow Him to transform and change me from the inside out. I strongly believe that if you don't have personal victory in your walk with God, you will have an extremely difficult time having victory in impacting the lives of others or in building an enduring ministry or work. Mature believers have learned the POWER of the **law of the Spirit of Life in Christ Jesus,** and they fight to help EVERY believer to **never move back to the law of sin and death.**

2) Higher Law 2 - The Law of Liberty and Grace

> "God forgives us, we must forgive ourselves. Otherwise, it is almost like setting up ourselves as a higher tribunal than Him."
>
> — C.S. Lewis

The Apostle Paul's main point in his New Testament letter to the Galatians is that EVERY human being is under a CURSE because of the Law of Moses. After giving more than 600 laws to the nation of Israel, Moses said the following:

> 'Cursed *is* the one who does not confirm all the words of this law by observing them' (Deuteronomy 27:26 NKJV).

Well, that means EVERYONE is under a CURSE from the Law of Moses.

The Bible says the ONLY one who can break that curse and set us free is Jesus.

> Christ has redeemed us from the curse of the law, having become a curse for us (for it is written, 'Cursed *is* everyone who hangs on a tree'), that the blessing of Abraham might come upon the Gentiles in Christ Jesus, that we might receive the promise of the Spirit through faith. (Galatians 3:13-14 NKJV).

Paul is very strong in his letter to the Galatians concerning the need for EVERY Christian to embrace a message based on GRACE not on keeping the law like in the Old Testament. Violating this law was in his eyes a SERIOUS offense:

> Let God's curse fall on anyone, including us or even an angel from heaven, who preaches a different kind of Good News than the one we preached to you. I say again what we have said before: If anyone preaches any other Good News than the one you welcomed, let that person be cursed. (Galatians 1:8-9 NLT).

This understanding is so critical to EVERY Christian because ONLY the Law of Liberty is able to BREAK the curse of the Old Testament LAW given by Moses and enable Christians to live in victory over that law. Paul goes on to write:

> Stand fast therefore in the **liberty** by which Christ has made us free, and do not be entangled again with a yoke of bondage. Indeed I, Paul, say to you that if you become circumcised, Christ will profit you nothing. And I testify again to every man who becomes circumcised that he is a debtor to keep the whole law. (Galatians 5:1–3 NKJV).

Here the apostle Paul is warning Christians NOT to be entangled again with bondage. This is in some ways connected with the law of sin and death whereby a Christian goes back to trying to "earn" their salvation by keeping God's Old Testament laws. Paul very clearly tells Christians to stay in GRACE. There is NO middle ground when it comes to keeping this law. Paul writes in the very next verse of Galatians 5:

> You have become estranged from Christ, you who *attempt* to be justified by law; you have **fallen from grace**. (Galatians 5:4 NKJV).

In James 1:25, the half brother of Jesus writes, "But he who looks into the **perfect law of liberty** and continues in it, and is not a forgetful hearer but a doer of the work, this one will be blessed in what he does."

There is a **law of liberty** in the New Testament that enables Christians to walk in freedom. We must keep this law because it is the secret to us walking in victory.

3) Higher Law 3 — The Law of Conscience

> "The needle of our conscience is as good a compass as any."
>
> — Ruth Wolff

> "He who has a fight with his conscience and loses, wins."
>
> — Unknown

The Apostle Paul deals with this law VERY clearly in his letter to the Corinthians:

Now regarding your question about food that has been offered to idols. Yes, we know that "we all have knowledge" about this issue. But while knowledge makes us feel important, it is love that strengthens the church. Anyone who claims to know all the answers doesn't really know very much. But the person who loves God is the one whom God recognizes.

So, what about eating meat that has been offered to idols? Well, we all know that an idol is not really a god and that there is only one God. There may be so-called gods both in heaven and on earth, and some people actually worship many gods and many lords. But for us,

> There is one God, the Father,
> by whom all things were created,
> and for whom we live.
> And there is one Lord, Jesus Christ,
> through whom all things were created,
> and through whom we live.

However, not all believers know this. Some are accustomed to thinking of idols as being real, so when they eat food that has been offered to idols, they think of it as the worship of real gods, and **their weak consciences are violated**. It's true that we can't win God's approval by what we eat. We don't lose anything if we don't eat it, and we don't gain anything if we do.

But you must be careful so that your freedom does not **cause others with a weaker conscience to stumble**. For if others see you—with your "superior knowledge"—eating in the temple of an idol, won't they be encouraged to **violate their conscience** by eating food that has been offered to an idol? So because of your superior knowledge, a weak believer for whom Christ died **will be destroyed**. And when you sin against other believers by encouraging them to do something they believe is wrong, you are sinning against Christ. So if what I eat causes another believer to sin, I will never eat meat again as long as I live—for I don't want to cause another believer to stumble.
(1 Corinthians 8:1–13 NLT).

Paul in this Scripture is dealing with food offered to idols, but he is actually dealing with a far more profound "law" that needs to govern EVERY mature believer. It is a nuanced relational sensitivity to NOT ONLY your OWN conscience, but ALSO to the conscience of another believer.

Basically, Paul is saying, just because something is OK for you to do, does NOT give you the license to do it. You can ONLY do it if it DOES NOT DAMAGE your brother or sister in Christ.

This takes great maturity because the New Testament law is greater and MORE difficult in many respects to keep than the Old Testament law. The New Testament requires a sensitive relationship to the Holy Spirit and to what grieves HIM and ALSO a sensitive relationship with OTHER BELIEVERS. Mature believers cannot be like bulls in a china shop and flaunt our freedom to those who might not yet be mature.

Two chapters later in his letter to the Corinthians, the Apostle Paul hits this same topic again.

> You say, "I am allowed to do anything"—but not everything is good for you. You say, "I am allowed to do anything"—but not everything is beneficial. Don't be concerned for your own good but for the good of others. So you may eat any meat that is sold in the marketplace **without raising questions of conscience.** For "the earth is the Lord's, and everything in it."
>
> If someone who isn't a believer asks you home for dinner, accept the invitation if you want to. Eat whatever is offered to you without raising questions of conscience. (But suppose someone tells you, "This meat was offered to an idol." Don't eat it, out of consideration for the conscience of the one who told you. It might not be a matter of conscience for you, but it is for the other person.) For why should my freedom be limited by what someone else thinks? If I can thank God for the food and enjoy it, why should I be condemned for eating it?
>
> So whether you eat or drink, or whatever you do, do it all for the glory of God. Don't give offense to Jews or Gentiles or the church of God. I too, try to please everyone in everything I do. I don't just do what is best for me; I do what is best for others so that many may be save (1 Corinthians 10:23–33 NLT).

Paul frequently tells mature believers to NOT get into quarreling and arguing over these matters of food and drink.

> Receive one who is weak in the faith, but not to disputes over doubtful things. For one believes he may eat all things, but he who is weak eats only vegetables. Let not him who eats despise him who does not eat, and let not him who does not eat judge him who eats; for God has received him. Who are you to judge another's servant? To his own master he stands or falls. Indeed, he will be made to stand, for God is able to make him stand (Romans 14:1–4 NKJV).

In the Old Testament, the laws of eating were VERY specific and eating the wrong food, or the wrong kind of animal or bird was a major sin. In Acts 10, the Apostle Peter has an experience where God drops down a large sheet filled with all kinds of unclean animals. God tells him to *"kill and eat."* When he protests that he has never eaten anything unclean, God says *"What God has cleansed you must not call common,"* (Acts 10:13 NKJV).

In the minds of most Christians, this experience of Peter settles the uncleanness issue when it comes to food, but Paul says that a lot of people will still stumble over this issue and it will seriously impact their faith. Paul says to not despise or judge a fellow believer because of food. It is NOT whether it is right or wrong, this law is one of conscience, and it DOES NOT ONLY PERTAIN TO FOOD. Paul writes:

> One person esteems one day above another; another esteems every day alike. Let each be fully convinced in his own mind. He who observes the day, observes it to the LORD; and he who does not observe the day, to the LORD he does not observe it. He who eats, eats to the LORD, for he gives God thanks; and he who does not eat, to the LORD he does not eat, and gives God thanks. For none of us lives to himself, and no one dies to himself. For if we live, we live to the LORD; and if we die, we die to the LORD. Therefore, whether we live or die, we are the LORD's. For to this end Christ died and rose and lived again, that He might be LORD of both the dead and the living. But why do you judge your brother? Or why do you show contempt for your brother? For we shall all stand before the judgment seat of Christ (Romans 14:5-10 NKJV).

In the Old Testament, it was very clear what was right or wrong, and most things were black and white. The New Testament requires great carefulness, great sensitivity, great wisdom and great relational insight to properly relate to people around you. Paul basically says you can eat pork but NOT if it causes someone to stumble. You can drink wine but NOT if it causes someone to stumble. You can celebrate any day of the week but NOT if it causes someone to stumble. You have to be sensitive NOT to violate your own conscience or the conscience of another believer. One needs to have at the center of one's thinking the health of the whole Body of Christ. One also needs to discern how mature and how ready others are to receive deeper and more profound teaching or understanding. Paul wrote again to the Corinthians:

> Dear brothers and sisters, when I was with you I couldn't talk to you as I would to spiritual people. I had to talk as though you belonged to this world or as though you were infants in Christ. I had to feed you with milk, not with solid food, because you weren't ready for anything stronger. And you still aren't ready (1 Corinthians 3:1–2 NLT).

Paul is basically saying that he wanted to share some really deep stuff with them but he couldn't because they were just NOT mature enough to handle it. This New Testament law is ALL ABOUT discerning your own conscience, the consciences of other people and their maturity levels. It requires a lot of personal maturity and relational wisdom and many Christians today have, unfortunately, NOT yet learned to walk in relational sensitivity and wisdom.

4) Higher Law 4 — The Law of Faith – shown by Action

> "When deeds speak, words are nothing."
>
> — African Proverb

In talking about the law of faith, I am NOT talking about salvation through faith NOR am I talking about growing in our trust and faith in Christ. Learning to trust Christ more every day and growing in your faith in His Word is a natural part of Christian growth. Scriptures such as Romans 10:17 which say, *"So then faith comes by hearing and hearing by the word of God,"* are foundational to a person's Christian life. That is not what I am focusing on with the law of faith.

The Apostle James, the half brother of Jesus, in his letter to the twelve tribes of Jewish believers, has many wonderful things to say about wisdom, endurance, and temptation.

He also, however, has a very strong message about faith versus works that many pastors often stumble over and have a hard time teaching to their congregations. Nobody should dispute whether Christians are saved by God's wonderful grace through faith in Jesus Christ. That is NOT what James is talking about when he speaks about faith and works. He is speaking about the lifestyle and behavior that will be the result of genuine true faith.

> What good is it, dear brothers and sisters, if you say you have faith but don't show it by your actions? Can that kind of faith save anyone? Suppose you see a brother or sister who has no food or clothing, and you say, "Good-bye and have a good day; stay warm and eat well"—but then you don't give that person any food or clothing. What good does that do? So you see, faith by itself isn't enough. Unless it produces good deeds, it is dead and useless. Now someone may argue, "Some people have faith; others have good deeds." But I say, "How can you show me your faith if you don't have good deeds? I will show you my faith by my good deeds" (James 2:14 NLT).

At the end of this chapter he sums up the whole matter: *"Just as the body is dead without breath, so also faith is dead without good works"* (James 2:26 NLT).

Mature believers need to develop more and more a love for others and a desire to help the poor, the needy and the less fortunate. The more the compassion of Christ impacts our lives, the more we want to help others practically.

I mentioned in chapter 4 that my home church is The Rock in San Bernardino, California. I also mentioned that the ones who started the church and the huge food outreach are Jim and Deby Cobrae, they have been like Mom and Dad to my wife Lisa and I. Jim has also, over the years, been my closest friend and I have witnessed first hand the love that he and Deby have for the less fortunate. It truly is the heart of Christ to care deeply for the hurting, the broken, the poor and the lost. Jim and Deby always challenge me in this area and provoke me to do more to help others.

Some years back we began sowing 10% of all the funds donated to our ministry into outreach and to be given to other ministries. We then took 10% of that amount and began giving it into Israel and into endeavors that help reach and bless the Jewish nation and especially Messianic believers. Although we very much need the donations of others, we have learned that we MUST continually become a conduit of blessing by faith to those less fortunate than ourselves.

In addition, we have created a **Thank God For Israel** fund and each year sow many thousands of dollars into the Holy Land and its people. So this compassion for the poor, needy and those close to God's heart is one side of the law of faith. God requires that true faith is backed up by genuine actions of caring and love towards others.

The second side of the law of faith is that you do things in life with a full assurance that you are not willfully violating God's will or God's ways in your personal conduct. This can literally be as broad as ANY action in life. Here is what the Apostle Paul writes about this:

> You may believe there's nothing wrong with what you are doing, but keep it between yourself and God. Blessed are those who don't feel guilty for doing something they have decided is right. But if you have doubts about whether or not you should eat something, you are sinning if you go ahead and do it. For you are not following your convictions. **If you do anything you believe is not right, you are sinning** (Romans 14:22–23 NLT).

The New King James Version simply says for this last verse, *"For whatever is not from faith is sin."*

So Paul is saying that living by faith is NOT simply having mental ascent towards a doctrine or creed or simply by accepting Christ as Savior. It is living in a way that shows the genuineness and depth of your beliefs in how you conduct your interactions with others, AND in the convictions, you adhere to in the ACTIONS of your everyday life. He says faith without corresponding ACTIONS is DEAD and that WHATEVER you do in life, you must have a full conviction that what you are doing is in the will of God.

5) Higher Law 5 — The Law of Love

> "We come to love not by finding a perfect person,
> but by learning to see an imperfect person perfectly."
>
> — Sam Keen

> "Love cures people - both the ones who give it
> and the ones who receive it."
>
> — Dr. Karl Menninger

CHAPTER 13: NEW TESTAMENT LAWS

The law of love is probably one of the most obvious of the New Testament laws. If there is ONE thing Jesus is known for, it's for His command to His disciples to love one another. All through the Gospel of John, the LOVE of Jesus for people and the world is clearly shown, and at the last supper, when Jesus is gathered with His disciples one final time before His horrendous crucifixion ordeal, He clearly gives this New Testament commandment using these words:

> A new commandment I give to you, that you love one another; as I have loved you, that you also love one another. By this all will know that you are My disciples, if you have love for one another (John 13:34–35 NKJV).

It is interesting that there is only ONE quality that Jesus said would be the hallmark of His disciples. He literally said the world would KNOW His true followers because of their LOVE for one another. It wasn't by how prosperous, joyful, musical or creative they would be. It wasn't even by how much faith they had, how many miracles they did, how much they did for the poor or how selfless they lived. It's not that any of these other things are bad, or that Christians should not do them, but by the words of Christ, these other qualities do NOT define a mature Christian. In one of the most famous chapters in the Bible (1 Corinthians 13), the Apostle Paul, in the midst of expounding on all the wonderful gifts of the Holy Spirit (chapters 12 and 14 of 1 Corinthians), hones in on, as he describes it, "a more excellent way" to live:

> Though I speak with the tongues of men and of angels, but have not love, I have become sounding brass or a clanging cymbal. And though I have the gift of prophecy, and understand all mysteries and all knowledge, and though I have all faith, so that I could remove mountains, but have not love, I am nothing. And though I bestow all my goods to feed the poor, and though I give my body to be burned, but have not love, it profits me nothing. Love suffers long and is kind; love does not envy; love does not parade itself, is not puffed up; does not behave rudely, does not seek its own, is not provoked, thinks no evil; does not rejoice in iniquity, but rejoices in the truth; bears all things, believes all things, hopes all things, endures all things. Love never fails (1 Corinthians 13:1–8 NKJV).

Most New Testament laws supersede or supplant previous Old Testament requirements. In many instances, they raise the bar. When it comes to the law of love, it is meant to actually help a person fulfill ALL the MANY commandments of the Old Testament law given by Moses. Here is how Paul describes the law of love.

Owe nothing to anyone—except for **your obligation to love one another**. If you love your neighbor, you will fulfill the requirements of God's law. For the commandments say, "You must not commit adultery. You must not murder. You must not steal. You must not covet." These—and other such commandments—are summed up in this one commandment: "Love your neighbor as yourself." **Love does no wrong to others, so love fulfills the requirements of God's law** (Romans 13:8–10 NLT).

6) Higher Law 6 — The Law of Perception

A *good* name is to be chosen rather than great riches
(Proverbs 22:1 NKJV)

God does care what the world thinks of Him, and He wants us to make sure we adorn the Gospel with a good reputation. The law of perception is subtle but nevertheless clearly described in the New Testament. Paul may not call some of these a LAW, but if the guideline of thinking and behavior is clearly articulated, I believe it is very appropriate for us to identify it as a New Testament LAW. Paul says one of the requirements for leadership is that a person has a good reputation:

So a church leader must be a man whose life is above reproach. He must be faithful to his wife. He must exercise self-control, live wisely, and have a good **reputation** (1 Timothy 3:2 NLT).

What Paul is talking about is the perception of others for a person being put in a place of leadership. They must be perceived to be people of high moral values and be well thought of by the church and also by the community.

The Apostle Paul was so sensitive to how he was perceived by others that he refused to take offerings for himself and he made sure that his preaching to them was not tainted by anything that could be misperceived to be an ulterior motive. This may seem like a small thing, but it was very sacrificial and meant he had to really stretch his faith for God's provision. Here is what Paul later wrote to the Corinthians:

Was I wrong when I humbled myself and honored you by preaching God's Good News to you without expecting anything in return? I "robbed" other churches by accepting their contributions so I could serve you at no cost. And when I was with you and didn't have enough

to live on, I did not become a financial burden to anyone.
(2 Corinthians 11:7–9 NLT).

If you read through the letters of Paul in the New Testament, he makes it very clear that he had every right to demand a financial return from the churches he planted but chose to not do so for ONE reason. He did not want anyone to accuse him of being a minister of the Gospel for financial gain. He was very sensitive to how his preaching ministry would be perceived.

I have two friends who live by this principle. One is Dave Hodgson, the billionaire businessman out of Australia who I talked about in an earlier chapter. He literally travels all over the world to speak at major Christian meetings and churches for ONE reason only, and that is to be obedient to God's mandate on his life to share his understanding in the marketplace with the Body of Christ. I know that in 2018, he spent over 3 million Australian dollars from his own resources to bring his message at no charge to others. He pays his own airfares and his own expenses just so he can stand before God's people and be free of ANY wrong perception. Paul writes in 1 Corinthians:

> If I were doing this on my own initiative, I would deserve payment. But I have no choice, for God has given me this sacred trust. What then is my pay? It is the opportunity to preach the Good News without charging anyone. That's why I never demand my rights when I preach the Good News (1 Corinthians: 9:17–18 NLT).

The second friend I have who does this is Jim Cobrae, whom I have mentioned several times throughout the book. He preached at a conference in Australia and was handed an honorarium of $20,000. He gave it back to the pastor who invited him and told him to invest it in God's Kingdom. Returning an honorarium has been more the norm in the ministry of both Jim and his wife Deby than the exception. They never want anyone perceiving them as being in the Gospel for money and purposely take steps to make sure that nobody gets the wrong impression.

Paul talked about doing everything he could to remove obstacles for people to accept Christ. He knew that people are naturally suspicious and most have many barriers to break through before they even listen to what you have to say. In the same chapter 9 of 1 Corinthians, which we just referenced, Paul goes on in the very next verses to describe his approach to reaching the lost world around him.

> Even though I am a free man with no master, I have become a slave to all people to bring many to Christ. When I was with the Jews, I lived like a Jew to bring the Jews to Christ. When I was with those who follow the Jewish law, I too lived under that law. Even though I am not subject to the law, I did this so I could bring to Christ those who are under the law. When I am with the Gentiles who do not follow the Jewish law, I too live apart from that law so I can bring them to Christ. But I do not ignore the law of God; I obey the law of Christ. When I am with those who are weak, I share their weakness, for I want to bring the weak to Christ. **Yes, I try to find common ground with everyone, doing everything I can to save some**. I do everything to spread the Good News and share in its blessings
> (1 Corinthians 9:19–23 NLT).

Paul is clearly referring to this law of perception when he speaks to Christians about the Holy Spirit gift of tongues, and he is also affirming that is a MATURE mindset:

> Brethren, do not be children in understanding; however, in malice be babes, but in understanding **be mature**. In the law it is written: "With men of other tongues and other lips I will speak to this people; And yet, for all that, they will not hear Me," says the LORD. Therefore tongues are for a sign, not to those who believe but to unbelievers; but prophesying is not for unbelievers but for those who believe. Therefore if the whole church comes together in one place, and all speak with tongues, and there come in those who are uninformed or unbelievers, will they not say that you are out of your mind?
> (1 Corinthians 14:20–23 NKJV).

Paul did not want Christians to be perceived as being weird or crazy. He wanted to minimize every barrier so that people would identify with him and hear his message.

This law of perception is a mindset that needs to govern the thinking of every mature Christian. Before he passed away, I twice heard Billy Graham talk about his greatest fear in life. He said that as he came to the end of his race, he feared more than anything that he would do something that would undo all the years of good ministry and integrity he had established and that he would somehow bring shame to the name of Christ and the message of the Gospel. This, to me, was a healthy fear.

Many times I hear crazy stories of Christian leaders who go through public divorces and who are back in the pulpit the following week. The divorce of one leader I know was literally the headlines in the Sunday papers of the nation where they were working. I am not so foolish as to believe that all divorce is unjustified. Certainly, there are some very painful situations of betrayal and heartbreak that people in leadership face, but seldom do I hear of people speaking about divorce from the point of view of how such public spectacles are perceived by the world and by the larger Body of Christ. God DOES care about how the world perceives Himself, His Church and those who represent Him. Everything we do MUST protect the Name of Christ, His reputation and His matchless message.

In the Old Testament, it was God's Name and reputation that Moses used to get God to change His plans and NOT to destroy the nation of Israel. After the children of Israel worshipped a golden calf at the base of Mount Sinai, Moses appealed to God's reputation with the Egyptians to try and save the nation of Israel from God's great anger against them.

> Then the LORD said, "I have seen how stubborn and rebellious these people are. Now leave me alone so my fierce anger can blaze against them, and I will destroy them. Then I will make you, Moses, into a great nation." But Moses tried to pacify the LORD his God. "O LORD!" he said. "Why are you so angry with your own people whom you brought from the land of Egypt with such great power and such a strong hand? **Why let the Egyptians say**, 'Their God rescued them with the evil intention of slaughtering them in the mountains and wiping them from the face of the earth'? Turn away from your fierce anger. Change your mind about this terrible disaster you have threatened against your people! Remember your servants Abraham, Isaac, and Jacob. You bound yourself with an oath to them, saying, 'I will make your descendants as numerous as the stars of heaven. And I will give them all of this land that I have promised to your descendants, and they will possess it forever.'" So the LORD changed his mind about the terrible disaster he had threatened to bring on his people
> (Exodus 32:9–14 NLT).

And the LORD said to Moses, "How long will these people treat me with contempt? Will they never believe me, even after all the miraculous signs I have done among them? I will disown them and destroy them with a plague. Then I will make you into a nation greater and mightier than they are!" But Moses objected. **"What will the Egyptians think when they hear about it?"** he asked the Lord. "They know full well the power you displayed in rescuing your people from Egypt. Now if you destroy them, the Egyptians will send a report to the inhabitants of this land, who have already heard that you live among your people. They know, Lord, that you have appeared to your people face to face and that your pillar of cloud hovers over them. They know that you go before them in the pillar of cloud by day and the pillar of fire by night. Now if you slaughter all these people with a single blow, the nations that have heard of your fame will say, 'The Lord was not able to bring them into the land he swore to give them, so he killed them in the wilderness.' "Please, Lord, prove that your power is as great as you have claimed. For you said, 'The Lord is slow to anger and filled with unfailing love, forgiving every kind of sin and rebellion. But he does not excuse the guilty. He lays the sins of the parents upon their children; the entire family is affected—even children in the third and fourth generations.' In keeping with your magnificent, unfailing love, please pardon the sins of this people, just as you have forgiven them ever since they left Egypt." Then the Lord said, "I will pardon them as you have requested. But as surely as I live, and as surely as the earth is filled with the Lord's glory (Numbers 14:11–21 NLT).

When it came to David's sin with Bathsheba, God did not allow that child out of wedlock to live, and there was ONE reason given. We find that reason in Nathan's prophesy to David concerning the child in 2 Samuel 12:

> So David said to Nathan, "I have sinned against the Lord." And Nathan said to David, "The Lord also has put away your sin; you shall not die. However, because by this deed **you have given great occasion to the enemies of the Lord to blaspheme**, the child also who is born to you shall surely die" (2 Samuel 12:13–14 NKJV).

God does care what the world thinks, and He does not want His Name to be blasphemed anywhere because of the actions of those who claim a faith in Him. God hates hypocrisy and is grieved by ANY behavior that shames His Name. Paul speaks about sexual immorality out of the same concern. He does highlight how it damages the individual believer and the temple of the Holy Spirit that every Christian has become, but he also points out how damaging it is to the message of Christ and to the perception of how the Church is perceived.

Sometimes we need to go out of our way to do what is acceptable in the sight of the world just to close down ANY criticism of the Church or the Gospel. God can certainly prosper Christian believers, but ALL Christians need to watch how their prosperity and lifestyle is perceived. The law of perception is simply a mindset that deeply cares about how the Church and the message of Christ are perceived. This is a MATURE Christian mindset.

While in one sense we don't want to offend the world, we have to be careful not to adopt worldy thinking when it comes to titles, dress, and relationships. The Jesus standard is to get a basin of water and wash the feet of those you serve. Paul, Timothy, and James all call themselves "slaves" of Jesus Christ. Christian leaders all too often get into competitive modes of thinking, comparing congregation sizes, skinny jeans, and hairstyles. One of the areas most documented in the New Testament is that of the disciples jockeying for positions of greatness and the rebukes Jesus gave them.

This brings me to another troublesome practice in God's Kingdom, and that is what I call "relationship ownership." It means that if I introduce you to someone, I somehow have a right to anything you do going forward with that person, especially financially. I know that's how the world often functions, but it should not be so in God's Kingdom. This is NOT how Jesus operated, and it does NOT follow the example He set for us. It often makes the Church seem very similar to secular business, which often requires a finder's fee.

While we are stepping on toes, we might as well delve in one more area of New Testament perception, and that is lawsuits. It's quite incredible how prevalent these are today and, from what we can read about in the Scriptures, this was an extremely big problem in the New Testament Church. Paul writes:

> When one of you has a dispute with another believer, how dare you file a lawsuit and ask a secular court to decide the matter instead of taking it to other believers! Don't you realize that someday we believers will judge the world? And since you are going to judge the world, can't you decide even these little things among yourselves? Don't you realize that we will judge angels? So you should surely be able to resolve ordinary disputes in this life. If you have legal disputes about such matters, why go to outside judges who are not respected by the church? I am saying this to shame you. Isn't there anyone in all the church who is wise enough to decide these issues? But instead, one believer sues another—right in front of unbelievers! Even to have such

lawsuits with one another is a defeat for you. Why not just accept the injustice and leave it at that? Why not let yourselves be cheated? Instead, you yourselves are the ones who do wrong and cheat even your fellow believers. Don't you realize that those who do wrong will not inherit the Kingdom of God? (1 Corinthians 6:1–9 NLT).

I understand this law of perception probably a little differently than most Americans. This is because I was required to go to a boarding school in South Africa from the age of seven until the age of 18. My high school was Hilton College, and it is one of the finest institutions of learning in southern Africa. Whenever a Hilton boy was out in public, he was always dressed in a school uniform with a tie and school blazer. It was drilled into us from the day we started school that we always represented the NAME of the school. If we misbehaved, it was not us as individuals that would be in the newspaper, and it would "a Hilton boy" that would be written about. The entire institution would be blamed for any infraction we made. Those in the US armed services would also greatly identify with this way of thinking.

We need to have a similar mentality concerning how we represent Christ. We cannot be so focused on our individual rights that we miss out on how our actions are perceived by those who know of our faith. I am somewhat ashamed to admit that this is a reason I don't have Christian bumper stickers on my car. Although I have a very good driving record, it is "in case" I make infractions on the road that might give Jesus a bad name.

A few other practical guidelines when it comes to this law of perception. We need to especially consider how our interactions with the opposite gender can be perceived. Whenever I have meetings with someone of the opposite sex, my office door is always open so that any member of my staff can walk in at any time and always see that nothing inappropriate is going on. Whenever possible, I try and do such meetings with my wife Lisa present or my daughter Christina (who is over 30 years old and a graduate of law school). I do my best to live very transparently before my wife, my staff, my board, and my family.

7) Higher Law 7 — The Law of Honor and Receiving

> "I've learned people will forget what you said, they will forget what you did, people will never forget how you made them feel."
>
> — Maya Angelou

The New Testament makes itclear that a person has to genuinely honor and respect things in order to partake of them. It is not enough to simply give mental assent to something. In order to really receive from God, there has to be a deep honoring of Him. This starts off with Christ Himself. Take these amazing words from John's Gospel about Jesus.

> He came unto his own, and his own received him not. **But as many as received him, to them gave he power** to become the sons of God, even to them that believe on his name: Which were born, not of blood, nor of the will of the flesh, nor of the will of man, but of God (John 1:10–13 NKJV).

It is amazing that God's Son was walking on the earth among humankind and that people saw his miracles and yet did not become children of God. He showed such love, such kindness, such genuine care and yet most of his family did NOT receive him. However, those who perceived His greatness honored His presence and embraced His love, to THEM He gave the power to become sons of God. If you do not perceive and honor the gift of God in another person, you CANNOT partake of that gift. In His teaching on earth, Jesus said the following:

> He who receives a prophet in the name of a prophet shall receive a prophet's reward. And he who receives a **righteous** man in the name of a **righteous** man shall receive a **righteous** man's reward (Matthew 10:41 NKJV).

When I was still a student at the University of Michigan, I started a small Bible study group in my campus dorm room. We ended up having an amazing group of about 12 college students who would show up at about 10 p.m. every Thursday night for a one hour Bible study. Because we often were doing street and outreach ministry, we sometimes would have a homeless person participate. That was how we discovered Meredith, a 40-year old fiery red-headed street person from the homeless population of Ann Arbor and the neighboring city of Ypsilanti.

Meredith was a fairly prolific smoker, and because of his life on the streets, he was unkempt and not exactly pleasantly scented. He had been rejected from a lot of churches but was, however, a genuine believer. As we honored him and made him feel loved and accepted, we discovered that he had an amazing prophetic spiritual gift. When God's presence came on him at the end of our Bible Study meetings, he would begin to prophesy over each attending member of the study. He was so accurate and 'read our mail' in a profound way. I cannot recall all the life-changing prophetic words that Meredith gave to us, but there were MANY. He was one of the most amazing gifts to the Church carefully disguised by God as a homeless person. We honored and received him and got to partake of the great gift of God in his life.

Probably the greatest way I learned this lesson happened soon after returning from our missionary work in Nigeria. The story started back in 1987 when Reinhard decided to do a fairly dangerous Gospel campaign in the northern region of Ghana in a city by the name of Tamale. It was dangerous because many of the people in that region were Muslims. It ended up being a spectacular crusade, and many of the miracles and preaching scenes featured in the movie *A Blood-Washed Africa* came from that campaign. My wife Lisa was, at that time, the journalist for Reinhard's ministry and she ran the publications department back in his office in Germany.

During one of the days we were there, Reinhard was invited to a village to meet a local chief. All of us went along, and because Lisa is short, all the village children were mobbing her; this is something that has been a constant in all the years I have known her. As we were making our way through the village, suddenly those in the front split to two sides of a deep prisoner pit. They often don't have jails in these villages but have about a nine-foot-deep smooth sided pit where they keep their miscreants. This is probably something similar to what Joseph in the Old Testament was thrown into by his brothers before being sold to the Ishmaelites in Genesis 37. Well, because the kids were blocking her way, Lisa saw the pit too late and fell headlong into it.

Because there was no rope or ladder to get her out, Reinhard had to have people holding on to his ankles, and he reached both hands into the pit to pull her out. What a picture of an evangelist! Literally pulling someone out of a deep pit. But somehow in that fall, Lisa damaged the left side of her body. From that day forward, she would often have severe pains in her left shoulder, sometimes in her left hip and often in her left breast. We knew we were in a strong environment of physical healing at Reinhard's crusades, but no healing manifested. In the next few years, we had huge events in Europe where Reinhard literally invited some of the most respected healing ministries from around the world to attend. Lisa frequently reached out to God for healing, but no healing came.

Lisa carried that pain through our time with Reinhard and then through two years at Fuller Seminary in Pasadena and then through two years on the mission fields of Nigeria. The pain was often severe, and I began to become worried about it. In 1994, we returned to California from Africa, and I already had drawn up a blueprint for the recordings to create the ISOM. I was so passionate about the vision that I wrote an article in a magazine called *Global Church Growth*. In the article, I described creating a missions tool that could bring Bible training to every nation of the world using the best teachers we could possibly find.

Soon after that article was published, I got a phone call from an elderly businessman in Singapore by the name of Leong Poe Lye. He said he had to fly over from Singapore and see me because of a dream he had confirmed what I had described in my article. He actually had seen an Olympic® Stadium where thousands of athletes were marching by with their flags, but they were not getting gold medals, they were receiving Bible School diplomas. He really felt my article was a confirmation of his dream. Brother Leong had a strange request when he spoke about flying to California to see me. He asked that I find some people with terminal illnesses because he said he had a grace on his life to pray for such cases.

Well, because I was an influential member of a large church, I did pull together a group of people needing prayer, and many of them were touched. After the prayer meeting, I invited him back to our small townhouse to meet my wife and young children. As brother Leong crossed the threshold of our back sliding door, I suddenly felt prompted to have him pray for Lisa. Lisa was in our living room, about 20 feet away. Brother Leong responded positively that he would love to pray for her and took a step towards her. Lisa knelt down on the small carpeting we had in the living room and, as she did, the power of God hit her and instantly healed her. Brother Leong never touched her or even got near to her. He simply took one small step towards her, and she was healed.

We were more than thrilled about the healing but also quite puzzled by this turn of events. I kept on wondering why the miracle had taken so long and why, when we were around so much healing, that Lisa was not healed in those meetings. About a month later, I was invited to minister with a lady by the name of Patricia Blue to a group of Russian leaders in Belgium. The former Soviet Union was really starting to open up, and the need for leadership training was huge.

After I poured out my heart to these leaders, the Russian brothers asked if they could pray for me. Of course, I obliged, but as they prayed for me, a different kind of anointing to any I had ever experienced came over me. I was questioning God about this different anointing when I felt Him clearly speak to my heart. I felt Him show me that He had purposely given different graces and giftings to different nations and peoples. Only as I opened myself for these Russian-speaking brothers to pray for me, could I partake of the anointing God had given them. Then I felt Him show me, brother Leong Poe Lye. God showed me how He had given the healing for my wife to this unlikely Chinese businessman from Singapore. Only as I had honored him and received him into my home, was I able to partake of that man's gift and immediately see my wife healed.

When you honor your leaders, then God can release great things into your life through them. When you become too familiar with them and lose that sense of honor, then it will begin to diminish what you can receive from them. Honoring, the Bible says, can also involve finances. Paul tells Timothy the following:

> Let the elders who rule well be counted worthy of double honor, especially those who labor in the word and doctrine
> (1 Timothy 5:17 NKJV).

Another version (NLT) for the first part of this verse simply says: *"Elders who do their work well should be respected and paid well."*

John Bevere has an amazing book titled *Honor's Reward*. I highly recommend it on this subject. The foundational principle of this higher law is to respect the person, the dignity, the gift and the calling of God in every believer. If you honor a servant of God, then you can partake of the gift of God that they carry, and it may be your miracle.

8) Higher Law 8 - The Law of Right Motive

> "Climb the mountain so you can see the world,
> not so the world can see you."
>
> — David McCullough Jr.
> (Commencement Address at Wellesley High School class of 2012)
>
> "You can give without loving, but you cannot love without giving."
>
> — Amy Carmichael

While I am sure there are many other laws that might be identified in the New Testament, I have really honed in on these eight strategic ones. The final law every mature believer needs to understand and function in is the law of right motive. Although God has always been interested in the motive of people's hearts, it is very evident in the New Testament that God was requiring a higher standard of truth and heart motivation. Many times in the Gospels, it records that Jesus knew what the people were thinking or He knew what was in their hearts. In His famous Sermon on the Mount, Jesus said the following:

> "You have heard that it was said to those of old, 'You shall not commit adultery.' But I say to you that whoever looks at a woman to lust for her has already committed adultery with her in his heart
> (Matthew 5:27–28 NKJV).

Here Jesus is not just focusing on the act of adultery but the thought or heart motivation of adultery. In many ways, Jesus upped the requirement and told us that, in order to be right with God, your motivations have to be genuine and full of truth. Nowhere is this more evident than in Acts 5 with the terrifying story of Ananias and his wife, Sapphira:

> But a certain man named Ananias, with Sapphira his wife, sold a possession. And he kept back part of the proceeds, his wife also being aware of it, and brought a certain part and laid it at the apostles' feet. But Peter said, "Ananias, why has Satan filled your heart to lie to the Holy Spirit and keep back part of the price of the land for yourself? While it remained, was it not your own? And after it was sold, was it not in your own control? Why have you conceived this thing in your heart? You have not lied to men but to God." Then Ananias, hearing these words, fell down and breathed his last. So great fear came upon all those who heard these things. And the young men arose and wrapped him up, carried him out, and buried him.
>
> Now it was about three hours later when his wife came in, not knowing what had happened. And Peter answered her, "Tell me whether you sold the land for so much?" She said, "Yes, for so much." Then Peter said to her, "How is it that you have agreed together to test the Spirit of the LORD? Look, the feet of those who have buried your husband are at the door, and they will carry you out." Then immediately she fell down at his feet and breathed her last. And the young men came in and found her dead, and carrying her out, buried her by her husband. So great fear came upon all the church and upon all who heard these things (Acts 5:1–10 NKJV).

Some people in the Church today have big debates over the tithe or over how much of a person's income needs to be given to God. These believers SOLD their house and probably gave a 90% offering to God of the proceeds. The issue was NOT the amount but was whether they gave the money with the right motivation and in TRUTH. They are accused of lying to the Holy Spirit, and it cost them their lives. While I believe in the tithe, the question is more for me that I bring an offering to God with a right heart and the right motivation.

Many years ago when I was on a missions trip to Spain, a young American missionary there shared with me an amazing true story that had taken place back in my home state of California. Apparently, in the city of Anaheim Hills, a godly female pastor had started a Japanese-speaking congregation. The church had grown well in a home environment, and the congregation was looking to buy or lease land so they could get their own building. It was at this time that a wealthy Japanese businessman attended the church. After a few weeks, he handed the pastor a check for $280,000. When she opened the check, she was initially thrilled at the size of the donation, but quickly she heard the LORD say to her: "Do not accept that donation, its given with a wrong heart and a wrong motivation."

She handed the large check back to the man and said, "I don't know why but God will NOT allow me to accept your donation." The man was offended and stormed away. Two weeks later he returned, and this time his entire demeanor had changed. He was weeping and crying with repentance and knelt down in front of the pastor and pleaded with her to please accept the donation. Only at that point did God give her the green light to accept the donation. It wasn't the amount that was the issue, and it was the heart behind the gift that mattered.

This issue is not just addressed to congregation members. The Apostle James writes the following to pastors and leaders in chapter 2 of his letter to the Jewish churches:

> My dear brothers and sisters, how can you claim to have faith in our glorious LORD Jesus Christ if you favor some people over others?
>
> For example, suppose someone comes into your meeting dressed in fancy clothes and expensive jewelry, and another comes in who is poor and dressed in dirty clothes. If you give special attention and a good seat to the rich person, but you say to the poor one, "You can stand over there, or else sit on the floor"- well, doesn't this discrimination show that **your judgments are guided by evil motives**?

> Listen to me, dear brothers and sisters. Hasn't God chosen the poor in this world to be rich in faith? Aren't they the ones who will inherit the Kingdom He promised to those who love Him? But you dishonor the poor! Isn't it the rich who oppress you and drag you into court? Aren't they the ones who slander Jesus Christ, whose noble name you bear?
>
> Yes indeed, it is good when you **obey the royal law as found in the Scriptures: "Love your neighbor as yourself."** But if you favor some people over others, you are committing a sin. You are guilty of breaking the law (James 2:1–9 NLT).

Here we get some crossover to the law of love. Many of these New Testament laws do overlap with each other, but the key factor here is the right motivation before God in how we deal with others. It is often such a subtle thing and an easy trap to fall into, but mature Christians MUST work on making sure their heart motivations stay pure in how they handle money, God's Word, and especially God's people. This is why I try and live in a very transparent way in my ministry. My wife and I do not like to hold secrets, and we do our level best to operate everything with open hands and an open heart. It is also why I try every year to take missions trips to places around the world that are less fortunate because it keeps my heart in the right place of loving the whole body of Christ.

This temptation towards favoritism and acting with wrong motivations is so subtle that even the Apostle Peter got confronted by the Apostle Paul for violating it in Galatians 2:

> But when Peter came to Antioch, I had to oppose him to his face, for what he did was very wrong. When he first arrived, he ate with the Gentile believers, who were not circumcised. But afterward, when some friends of James came, Peter wouldn't eat with the Gentiles anymore. He was afraid of criticism from these people who insisted on the necessity of circumcision. As a result, other Jewish believers followed Peter's hypocrisy, and even Barnabas was led astray by their hypocrisy: When I saw that they were not following the truth of the Gospel message, I said to Peter in front of all the others, "Since you, a Jew by birth, have discarded the Jewish laws and are living like a Gentile, why are you now trying to make these Gentiles follow the Jewish traditions? "You and I are Jews by birth, not 'sinners' like the Gentiles. Yet we know that a person is made right with God by faith

in Jesus Christ, not by obeying the law. And we have believed in Christ Jesus, so that we might be made right with God because of our faith in Christ, not because we have obeyed the law. For no one will ever be made right with God by obeying the law." But suppose we seek to be made right with God through faith in Christ and then we are found guilty because we have abandoned the law. Would that mean Christ has led us into sin? Absolutely not! Rather, I am a sinner if I rebuild the old system of law I already tore down (Galatians 2:11–18 NLT).

We see that even Barnabas got sucked into this human tendency and again we see a crossover between this law and the law of liberty and grace. Jesus came to break off from us the human tendency to discriminate based on looks, race, gender, and class. As Paul wrote in Galatians:

For you are all children of God through faith in Christ Jesus. And all who have been united with Christ in baptism have put on Christ, like putting on new clothes. There is no longer Jew or Gentile, slave or free, male and female. For you are all one in Christ Jesus (Galatians 3:26–28 NLT).

Million Pound Joke

"Do not judge by appearances; a rich heart may be under a poor coat."

— Scottish Proverb

Many years ago, when I was working with Reinhard Bonnke, I got to film a young evangelist and musician in England by the name of Ray Bevan. I actually went into a British school and watched this very amusing and talented guy do a school assembly. He had the kids rolling in the aisles with laughter and then he took out his guitar and began to sing and minister life to those youngsters. I remember how the power of God touched those kids as Ray sang his closing song, which was a Scott Wesley Brown song titled "This Little Child." As Ray closed out with prayer, many of those kids came to faith in Christ, and many of them had tears in their eyes after that short 20-minute time of testimony and ministry.

Years later Ray started a wonderful church in Newport, Wales called *The Kings Church*, which, after pastoring for 25 years, he transitioned over to Dave and Faye Edwards in 2014. I mention Ray because, in 1992, Reinhard Bonnke did this huge project in England where he sent a beautiful booklet explaining the Gospel to every home in the country - like 25 million booklets. He needed about six million British pounds or about 10 million US dollars to pay for the project. Time was running out and the money needed did not seem to be coming in. Reinhard was going from church to church in England encouraging the Body of Christ to get behind the project. It was during that time that Reinhard found himself preaching at *The King's Church*.

As I previously mentioned, Ray is a crazy funny guy who often makes jokes. That evening when Ray took the offering, he was cracking jokes, and while asking people to support Reinhard's project, he said, "There is probably somebody here who could give a million pounds, and it would not even hurt you." Well nobody gave a million pounds but after the service this really badly dressed man came up to Ray as he was leaving the meeting and asked if anyone had given a million pounds. Ray looked at him and said in his thick Welsh accent, "It was a blinkin' joke, sir."

The man looked like a tramp or a street person, but he said, "I would like to speak to Reinhard Bonnke." Ray looked at the unkempt man and told him Reinhard was busy having tea right then. He did not respect this homeless looking character, but as Ray was leaving to join Reinhard for tea, the man asked where Reinhard was staying, and Ray shouted to him the hotel name there in Newport, Wales.

That night, at about 11 PM the man called Reinhard in his hotel room from the lobby downstairs. At first, the man would not give his name but just requested the opportunity to ask Reinhard some questions. Reinhard respected him, and for about 20 minutes he answered all the man's questions. Then he told Reinhard his name. Reinhard said on the phone, "I know you, sir, I know you." The man said he did not know Reinhard and that Reinhard must be mistaken. Reinhard answered, "I just finished reading a book on the 100 wealthiest people in the UK and, you sir, you are number 20 (the 20th richest person in the UK)." The man said he was touched that a German person was doing something to reach the British people (considering the history between the two nations). He said he was going to give a million pounds to Reinhard. Five days later, the money dropped into Reinhard's Christ for All Nations UK ministry account. That story unlocked a tidal wave of giving in England and during the next few weeks over 6 million pounds came in, enabling Reinhard to meet the budget, pay the postage and send out all the salvation booklets. Hundreds of thousands of decisions for Christ was the result.

Later Reinhard asked the man why he dressed so badly. His answer was very revealing. He said he "always dressed down (badly) so he could see what was in people's hearts" when they spoke to him. From what I understand, he never went back to that church because Ray had not honored him. The funny thing is that I heard this true story directly from Reinhard and subsequently also from Ray Bevan. Ray says many times since then he has said the same words that someone in the audience probably could give a million pounds and it would not even hurt them, but the money has never again been forthcoming.

CHAPTER FOURTEEN

Going on to Full Maturity

We have looked at many different facets of the maturing process but where does it all lead and what does full maturity look like? Let's start with 2 Peter 1:3–11. I have added the numbering into this Scripture to clarify the maturing process that Peter is speaking about. He has put these additions to faith into a very deliberate sequence that will result in a person **never falling away from their faith**.

> By his divine power, God has given us everything we need for living a godly life. We have received all of this by coming to know him, the one who called us to himself by means of his marvelous glory and excellence. And because of his glory and excellence, he has given us great and precious promises. These are the promises that enable you to share his divine nature and escape the world's corruption caused by human desires.
>
> In view of all this, make every effort to respond to God's promises. **Supplement your faith** with:
>
> 1) a generous provision of moral excellence, and
> 2) moral excellence with knowledge, and
> 3) knowledge with self-control, and
> 4) self-control with patient endurance, and
> 5) patient endurance with godliness, and
> 6) godliness with brotherly affection, and
> 7) brotherly affection with love for everyone.
>
> The more you grow like this, the more productive and useful you will be in your knowledge of our LORD Jesus Christ. But those who fail to develop in this way are shortsighted or blind, forgetting that they have been cleansed from their old sins. So, dear brothers and sisters, work hard to prove that you really are among those God has called and chosen. **Do these things, and you will never fall away.** Then God will give you a grand entrance into the eternal Kingdom of our LORD and Savior Jesus Christ (2 Peter 1:3–11 NKJV).

So it is obvious from this Scripture that the foundation of our walk with Christ is FAITH. Peter says that we need to add to this moral excellence, which also is translated in other places as *virtue*. The original Greek says virtue means moral goodness and uprightness. Here is how the sequence reads in the Amplified version:

For this very reason, applying your diligence [to the divine promises, make every effort] in [exercising] your faith to, develop moral excellence, and in moral excellence, knowledge (insight, understanding), and in your knowledge, self-control, and in your self-control, steadfastness, and in your steadfastness, godliness, and in your godliness, brotherly affection, and in your brotherly affection, [develop Christian] love [that is, learn to unselfishly seek the best for others and to do things for their benefit] (2 Peter 1:5–7 AMP).

The reason this book is titled PURSUING Maturity is because there is a process, a sequence and a journey that every Christian has to go through to arrive at a place where they will become mature and **will never fall away**. It is NOT automatic, and it takes the focus and preparation of an athlete, the strength, discipline, and courage of a soldier and the patience and hard work of a farmer to run with endurance to a finish line. Twice in the New King James Version, it uses the word DILIGENCE:

Verse 5	But also for this very reason, **giving all diligence**, add to your faith . . .
Verse 10	Therefore, brethren, be **even more diligent** to make your call and election sure . . .

This means there is an intensity, an intentionality, and a carefulness to make sure we pursue this sequence that Peter lays out for us.

In the USA there is a very popular show called the *Amazing Race*. Here is how Wikipedia® describes this race:

"The Amazing Race is a reality television game show in which teams of two people race around the world in competition with other teams. Contestants strive to arrive first at "Pit Stops" at the end of each leg of the race to win prizes and to avoid coming in last, which carries the possibility of elimination or a significant disadvantage in the following leg. Contestants travel to and within multiple countries in a variety of transportation modes, including: airplanes, hot air balloons, helicopters, trucks, bicycles, taxicabs, cars, trains, buses, boats, and by foot. Clues provided in each leg lead the teams to the next destination or direct them to perform a task, either together or by a single member. These challenges are related in some manner to the country wherein they are located or its culture. Teams are progressively eliminated until three are left; at that point, the team that arrives first in the final leg is awarded the grand prize."

This show, to me, is like a micro version of the Christian race. We have a goal and a prize that we are after. In the Amazing Race, the grand prize is most often US $1 million. Our prize is eternal life and a reward beyond our imagination. We have many stages of this race, and the Apostle Peter lays those out for us in 2 Peter 1. We don't want to be eliminated, so we must follow the clue book God has given, which is the Word of God. The journey is often difficult and has many twists and turns, but we need to stay on track. Our ONE difference is that we don't want others eliminated, but want to help everyone to cross that finish line and receive a full reward.

The end goal here on earth is godly Christian LOVE built upon moral character, self-control, steadfastness, knowledge, and faith. It is an ever-ascending journey to a higher place of intimacy with Christ and a place of stability and fruitfulness in His harvest and His Kingdom. Peter says that if Christians follow this sequence, the following will happen: *The more you grow like this, the more productive and useful you will be in your knowledge of our Lord Jesus Christ* (2 Peter 1:8 NLT). In other words, you will become mature and productive in God's Kingdom. This is the goal of God for EVERY Christian.

Trials, Hardships, and Persecution
I would do everyone a disservice if I gave the impression that maturity was possible without great opposition, trial, hardship and often, persecution. One of the prayers I pray daily is "Lord help me to finish well." This is because I have studied so many of the Kings in the Old Testament and found that very few finished well. Even Solomon, who asked for so much wisdom, ended up messing up his life with sin at the end.

I also realized that out of more than one million Hebrews who left Egypt for the Promised Land with Moses, only TWO (Joshua and Caleb) made it in. That entire story is a picture of the Christian walk with Jesus being the Passover Lamb, the blood on the doorposts in the shape of a cross saving the firstborn children, the water baptism symbolized by the Red Sea crossing, the manna in the wilderness being our daily bread of God's Word taught by Jesus in the Lord's Prayer, and many other types and shadows. The Promised Land was their destination. Ours is finishing well, with maturity in our lives, taking territory for God and getting a full reward.

As I look through the Bible and evaluate who finished well, it seems that there were two recognizable factors. The first factor was strong mentorship and the second factor was strong affliction. The following people who finished well seem to fit into one of those two categories and some had both. I am speaking about people like Noah, Abraham, Jacob, Joseph, Moses, Joshua, Ruth, Samuel, Elijah, Elisha, Daniel, Esther, King David, the apostles Paul, Peter, James, John and of course, Jesus. These were some of the great finishers of the Scriptures. I do know that in our ministry, God put Lisa and me with Reinhard Bonnke as a great mentor but He then sent us out as missionaries for a grueling two years in Nigeria. This was at a time when there was a lot of unrest and killing happening in the northern Nigeria region where we lived between the Christians and the Muslims. He forged our faith in a difficult place.

There is no question that David in the Bible had great mentorship in the house of Saul as he played his harp before the King. Then for many years, he had to run for his life and trust God every day for survival in the caves and the forests of the countryside. The same was true with Joseph who had to endure difficult tests as a slave separated from his family in the house of Potiphar, and then in a dungeon for maintaining his integrity with Potiphar's wife. God tested his faithfulness and his walk with God.

The New Testament shares the same pattern, and the lists of trials and afflictions that the Apostle Paul went through are quite incredible (some are listed in 2 Corinthians 11:22–33). Of the 12 original Apostles that functioned in the book of Acts, with the replacement Apostle Matthias mentioned in Acts 1, only ONE (John) made it to old age, and 11 ended up being martyred for their faith. James, the half brother of Jesus, Paul and Peter all speak to the area of trials and afflictions in the Christian life. Here is a classic verse:

> My brethren, count it all joy when you fall into various trials, knowing that the testing of your faith produces patience. But let patience have its perfect work, that you may be **perfect and complete**, lacking nothing (James 1:2–4 NLT).

Again we see the result of trials, which is MATURITY (perfect and complete). Peter says it like this:

> In this you greatly rejoice, though now for a little while, if need be, you have been **grieved by various trials**, that the genuineness of your faith, being much more precious than gold that perishes, **though it is tested by fire**, may be found to praise, honor, and glory at the revelation of

Jesus Christ, whom having not seen you love. Though now you do not see Him, yet believing, you rejoice with joy inexpressible and full of glory, receiving the end of your faith—the salvation of your souls (1 Peter 1:6–9 NKJV).

Here again, we see that our faith is like precious gold and that trials are like a purifying fire to bring us to a place where our lives will be to the praise, honor, and glory of God when Jesus is revealed to the world. It also solidifies our salvation because the *"end of our faith"* according to Peter will be *"the salvation of our souls."* The Apostle Paul shows that he has learned through his incredible trials and experiences that NOTHING can separate a Christian from God's love:

> Who shall separate us from the love of Christ? Shall tribulation, or distress, or persecution, or famine, or nakedness, or peril, or sword? As it is written: "For Your sake we are killed all day long; We are accounted as sheep for the slaughter." Yet in all these things we are more than conquerors through Him who loved us. For I am persuaded that neither death nor life, nor angels nor principalities nor powers, nor things present nor things to come, nor height nor depth, nor any other created thing, shall be able to separate us from the love of God which is in Christ Jesus our Lord (Romans 8:35–39 NKJV).

Paul is basically saying here that no matter what trial, what tribulation, what persecution or what distress you confront as a Christian, NOTHING can separate us from Christ's love. It is just a fact that part of the maturing process as a Christian is to face every kind of opposition and to discover that Christ is ABLE to be with you and help you no matter what you are encountering.

Because of the work we do in Asia, I have had the privilege of ministering to many believers in persecuted nations. In the past few years, one of those nations passed some new draconian laws making it illegal for me to minister to those believers. That is NOT a law that governments have the authority to make. Caesar's jurisdiction does not dictate what is to happen in God's Kingdom and in His Church. The law mandated a heavy fine if any contact was made with foreign Christians.

While I was there, the leader of the movement stood up and announced the new situation. He then said that if they had a large fine imposed on them, they would not pay it and he was fully ready to go to jail again if he had to. This particular individual had been many times in prison already. I remember being so struck with the fearlessness of these believers. They fully understood the words of Paul in Romans 8. They did not love their own lives and were ready at any time to pay the highest price for their faith.

Experience
A final facet of this maturing process is experience. I remember a pastor in Michigan telling the story of a community in Canada that, many years ago, had purchased a new generator to supply power for their city. They purchased the large piece of equipment from a generator company in California. This beautiful new generator worked perfectly for about three years but then, one morning, it suddenly made strange sounds, seized up and stopped working.

The local electricians, engineers, and technicians in that small town tried for two hours to discover the problem but had NO clue why the machine had ceased working. By lunchtime, they made an emergency decision to pay for a private jet to fly a mature technician up to Canada from the company in California that had sold them the machine. The man was found and flew up to Canada, arriving at about 5 p.m. Not wanting their city to spend the night in darkness, the California technician was rushed to the generator room.

While all the local experts watched, the California technician spent 10 minutes systematically checking from one side of the large machine to the other. After 10 minutes, he requested a large screwdriver. When they hastily gave him one, he turned the screwdriver around, holding it by the metal portion. He then took a giant step towards the machine and sharply hit the machine with the reverse side of the screwdriver. The people in the room were astonished at his actions, but he turned to the local technician and asked him to turn on the key to the machine. It roared to life, and the machine now functioned again perfectly. All in the room were baffled by what had happened but gratefully took the California expert back to the airport where he was flown back to his headquarters.

Imagine the shock up in Canada when the bill arrived for the visit. The city in Canada had already paid a small fortune for the private charter plane to bring the expert from California. The invoice only had ONE line. It simply read: "For fixing your generator - $5,010."

The leaders in Canada were incensed. The California company was charging $5,010 for hitting their generator with the back end of a screwdriver and a 10-minute visit. They sent an angry letter back to the California company demanding an itemized breakdown of the invoice. Two weeks later a second invoice arrived from California. This time it had TWO lines. The first line said "$10 – for hitting your generator with a screwdriver." The second line read "$5,000 – for knowing WHERE to hit the generator with the screwdriver."

There is something about being in situations that put a demand on your talents and gifts. When I was a children's pastor with 1,200 kids needing attention, my ministry gifts to children became incredibly well honed. I learned how to quiet down a group of 500 rowdy kids in just a few seconds. I learned how to control lights, music, and atmosphere to maximize the impact of a message on those kids. When I was with Reinhard, I watched how adept he was at ministering to massive crowds. It was through extensive use of his gifts that he had become MATURE in using them and was able to bring millions to Christ each year.

The main point to remember with experience is that Christians need to become, with the help of God, the greatest specialists in every possible area of life. There is huge value in becoming competent and adept in whatever profession we are called to. The Bible says our gift will make room for us (Proverbs 18:16). Daniel got access to the throne of Babylon through his gift at discerning dreams. Joseph went from the prison to the palace for the same reason. Both also had greatly developed their administrative skills and were able to manage projects far more ably than anyone else. Young David's skill on the harp gave him entrance into Saul's palace, and his gift at using a slingshot helped him bring down Goliath.

Discernment

The writer of Hebrews inserts this gem into that book:

> Solid food is for those who are **mature**, who through training have the skill to recognize the difference between right and wrong.
> (Hebrews 5:14 NLT)

> But strong meat is for the **perfect**; for them who by custom have their senses exercised to the discerning of good and evil.
> (Hebrews 5:14 Douay-Rheims)

In this Hebrews 6 Scripture, the emphasis is not just on being skilled in using a spiritual gift or even a natural gift. It is on being able to handle weighty topics and SOLID MEAT when it comes to the deeper mysteries of the Bible. The writer of Hebrews says that MATURE believers can discern whether deeper profound teachings are from God or NOT. Maturity in a Christian brings greater discernment and when it comes to types and shadows and hidden meanings, this type of maturity is greatly needed. The Apostle Paul touches on some of these deep truths, but many times he backs away from sharing because he does not think there is enough maturity on the receiving side. Even books like the Book of Revelation need people with great maturity to decipher them.

The one factor when it comes to experience and discernment is the TIME it takes for an individual to come to maturity. Paul wrote to Timothy that he was NOT to put people into leadership too early. This is how he said it:

> A church leader must not be a new believer, because he might become proud, and the devil would cause him to fall (1 Timothy 3:6 NLT).

I am always counseling mature people to consider how long it took for them to become stable and steadfast in their walk with God, to stop being double-minded and to get their own ego out of the way of their faith. When we were developing the ISOM, we recorded roughly 100 sessions of usable training during the first year. I was tired, and we had almost no money. I remember thinking that surely 100 sessions of teaching was going to be enough. I hardly thought people would take the time to listen to those, never mind any others. It was at that time that I felt the LORD showed me that it took God in the flesh (Jesus) over three years to prepare 11 people BEFORE He gave them the Great Commission. The indication was that there was NO SHORTCUT to making a disciple and that we were NOT going to bypass the process.

If we look at the whole chapter in 1 Timothy 3, Paul is saying people should not be appointed to leadership unless they have certain qualities. As we close out this chapter and move to a conclusion of this book, I would like you to look at ALL we have discussed about what maturity looks like in an individual and see how it matches up with Paul's recommended qualities for leaders:

> This is a trustworthy saying: "If someone aspires to be a church leader he desires an honorable position." So a church leader must be a man whose life is above reproach. He must be faithful to his wife. He must exercise self-control, live wisely, and have a good reputation. He must enjoy having guests in his home, and he must be able to teach. He must not be a heavy drinker or be violent. He must be gentle, not quarrelsome, and not love money. He must manage his own family well, having children who respect and obey him. For if a man cannot

manage his own household, how can he take care of God's church? A church leader must not be a new believer, because he might become proud, and the devil would cause him to fall. Also, people outside the church must speak well of him so that he will not be disgraced and fall into the devil's trap (1 Timothy 3:1–7 NLT).

Paul is saying to appoint MATURE believers into positions of leadership in the church. Well-rounded maturity should be the most important ingredient in any person aspiring to a position of leadership in God's Church.

CHAPTER FIFTEEN

A Loyal Heart

"I'll take fifty percent efficiency to get one hundred percent loyalty."

— Samuel Goldwyn

I started off early in this book by stating the following: "What are the practical elements or ingredients that will help believers to become mature?" The goal before us is to help mold into the lives of people true Christian character and to set individuals on a pathway to fulfilling their calling.

What follows is how I phrased the need in the Body of Christ:

> "We need a generation of believers who are full of conviction but not legalistic, bold but not brash, strong but yet gentle. We need multifaceted Christians who are cognizant of their callings, full of vision and purpose, able to articulate their faith and ideas while understanding and respecting the positions and perspectives of others. We need those who can intelligently express their intellect and their emotions and whose lives reflect the genuine fruit of God's Spirit without hypocrisy or double-mindedness."

Well, there is just ONE last quality I want to add into the mix of all that I have said, and that is **loyalty of heart**. There is a reason why God's Word says the following:

> For the eyes of the LORD run to and fro throughout the whole earth, to show Himself strong on behalf of those whose heart is loyal to Him (2 Chronicles 16:9 NKJV).

The word for loyal is *shalem*, which means "perfect, complete (of keeping covenant relation) peace (of covenant of peace, mind) safe, peaceful, perfect, whole, full, at peace."

Does that word 'perfect' trigger something in your mind from all the chapters you have read in this book? This word *shalem* is mentioned 27 times in the Scriptures. The meanings carry with them the idea of serving God with a sincere heart, a covenant keeping heart, a single-minded and loyal devotion. It also conveys the clear idea of serving God with all your heart, with full love, loyalty, and integrity.

A few years ago I was in my office in Redlands, California when the telephone rang. One of the ladies in my office answered it and came running through to where I was. "It's Reinhard Bonnke," she said excitedly. At that particular time, I had not worked for Reinhard in over 25 years. I had not spoken to him in three or four years, as I tried hard not to bother him, knowing how much his time was always in demand. I was surprised to hear from him, but within seconds I could sense that the love and friendship I had always enjoyed with him was there. Reinhard said, "Berin, I have a donor who wants to give $50,000 away to a worthy ministry and this person has asked me to recommend somebody. I would like to recommend your ministry."

Now $50,000 may seem like a huge amount, but it's about what our ministry uses in a week. What thrilled me more than the amount, was the fact that of all the ministries Reinhard knows, he recommended ours. It was then that I understood something about loyalty of heart. I knew I had served Reinhard as a spiritual son with ALL my heart, with full commitment and devotion, and that all these years later, that loyalty was being rewarded. I truly believe that God will ALWAYS reward and do great things for someone with a LOYAL HEART.

From that 2 Chronicles 16:9 Scripture we see that God searches the WHOLE EARTH looking for this ONE quality in a human being. When He finds it, and He is definitely looking for it, then He will show Himself STRONG on behalf of that person.

One of the greatest examples in Scripture of a person with a totally loyal heart is the Old Testament story of Ruth. You often cannot tell true loyalty until it is tested. Ruth's loyalty is shown after total tragedy in her life and in the life of the family she was a part of. She grew up in the nation of Moab, a foreign land that was NOT a part of the promises of God to Israel.

Ruth's mother in law, Naomi, had moved to the land of Moab with her husband Elimelech and her two sons Mahlon and Chilion because of a famine in Israel. They had come from Bethlehem, the future birthplace of Jesus. What happened then was an absolute disaster. Elimelech tragically died in Moab. The two sons then took wives from the people of Moab, and the wives names were Orpah and Ruth. It was not long before tragedy struck again and Mahlon died. Soon after that, Chilion died and left Naomi with two widowed daughters-in-law. This all happened within a seven-year period.

With dreams and hopes shattered, Naomi makes the decision to return to Bethlehem. She tells the daughters-in-law to go back to their people and to try and find other husbands. It is in the midst of all this sorrow and pain that we get one of the most powerful illustrations of loyalty of heart in ALL of Scripture. Here is how Ruth speaks to Naomi:

> But Ruth replied, "Don't ask me to leave you and turn back. Wherever you go, I will go; wherever you live, I will live. Your people will be my people, and your God will be my God. Wherever you die, I will die, and there I will be buried. May the LORD punish me severely if I allow anything but death to separate us!" (Ruth 1:16-17 NKJV)

I believe the eyes of the LORD honed in on this beautiful Moabite heart and God decided to show Himself strong on her behalf. He took her from Moab and planted her in Bethlehem, and she ended up becoming a part of the lineage of King David and eventually of Jesus the Messiah.

The book of Proverbs in the New Living Translation has a very insightful comment on the quality of loyalty: *"Loyalty makes a person attractive"* (Proverbs 19:22 NLT).

Hachiko, the Japanese dog

A few years ago I led a missions trip to Tokyo, Japan. As we came out of one of the major metro train stations in Tokyo, we came across a bronze statue of a dog. This dog, whose name was Hachiko used to meet his master at that train station every evening when he came back from work. His master was a teacher and professor by the name of Professor Ueno, a professor of agriculture at the University of Tokyo. One day while at work, Professor Ueno had a brain hemorrhage and died. He never returned home after that, but the dog for the next nine years, until it died, would appear at that same spot every evening at the exact time that his master's train used to arrive. The people of Japan were so moved by the loyalty of this dog that they have erected three bronze statues of Hachiko, and the story of the dog's loyalty has inspired at least two movies. In John 10:11-16 Jesus compares the loyalty of shepherd with the loyalty of a hireling:

> I am the good shepherd. The good shepherd sacrifices his life for the sheep. A hired hand will run when he sees a wolf coming. He will abandon the sheep because they don't belong to him and he isn't their shepherd. And so the wolf attacks them and scatters the flock. The hired hand runs away because he's working only for the money and doesn't really care about the sheep. I am the good shepherd; I know my

own sheep, and they know me, just as my Father knows me and I know the Father. So I sacrifice my life for the sheep. I have other sheep, too, that are not in this sheepfold. I must bring them also. They will listen to my voice, and there will be one flock with one shepherd
(1 John 10:11–16 NKJV).

The shepherd cares, is willing to fight, to protect, to love and even to die for the sheep. The hireling doesn't care but runs from trouble and is only interested in themselves. Those who are mature must develop the heart of a shepherd.

A loyal heart is a vulnerable heart. It can be wounded because it is kept tender. It's a heart that always believes, never quits, never stops caring, never stops loving, never stops trying. It has a singular focus and is NOT double-minded. When God sees that kind of heart, and He is looking for it, then He will move into action on your behalf.

I truly believe that this quality of loyalty is the ultimate crowning jewel of a mature Christian. It is why 11 of the 12 original disciples of Jesus were willing to be martyred. It is the ultimate antidote to betrayal, and it is the bedrock of solid marriages, friendships, and relationships. It may take some years, but I believe God will always reward this mature quality.

CONCLUSION

After all the chapters in this book, I pray it is clear that maturity is a multi-faceted nuanced state of being. It is complex yet principled. It is certainly NOT just a set of rules that someone religiously follows. I believe when you see maturity, it can be easily recognized, just like when you see a mature musician, athlete, or doctor. Maturity in a Christian looks like Jesus in the Gospels. You see someone loving and caring, but uncompromising and unafraid of the truth. You see someone who is led by the Holy Spirit, but deeply and practically engaged with the people around them. Most of all, you see someone completely free of hypocrisy, living transparently from their heart and clear in their purpose in life.

People get to that place of maturity through a series of defining moments that set the course of their lives. They passionately pursue a relationship with God, seeking to know Him and His will for their lives. They embrace a God-identity, learning to fear Him and cognizant that they were uniquely created for a purpose and a calling. They then seek out the vehicles of process that will mold and develop their character, talent, and relational opportunities. All of these decisions they lay on God's altar and seek wisdom from the Holy Spirit before making them.

These people pursuing maturity are willing to find godly mentors whom they choose to live before in a transparent way. They are passionate about revelation understanding from God's Word and learn to recognize such teaching by the obvious fruit it bears in the lives of those teaching it. They are passionate about truth and fully embrace God's Word as the rock on which everything in their life is built. They keep adding, step by step, pieces to their lives that develop them along the lines of 2 Peter 1. They learn that trials and persecution are simply tools God uses to help sculpt their character, their patience, and their endurance. More and more, they learn to live in relationship with God and with others, blessing their enemies, forgiving everyone daily, and loving their brothers and sisters in Christ passionately but appropriately.

As these saints grow closer to their goal of maturity, they learn to die to self, and they become more and more intimate with the Savior and with His precious Holy Spirit. They develop godly disciplines and learn a deep sensitivity to the perceptions of others. They create as few obstacles to the Gospel as possible and build as many bridges into the lives of others as they can. They learn the power of the words of an African proverb, which says, "When deeds speak, words are nothing." What St. Francis of Assisi said: "It is no use walking anywhere to preach unless our walking is our preaching." These believers understand how to live in a balanced and a nuanced way, respecting their own conscience and the conscience of others.

Finally, these maturing saints understand their authority as God's representatives even though they walk in increasing humility. They believe in the power of God, and they see God supernaturally help them in every facet of their lives. They increasingly get ideas from heaven and experience extraordinary favor in seeing those God-ideas come to fruition. They recognize Christ's Lordship over everything they have and have no problems bringing a tenth of what they earn back to God. They give generously to missions, the poor, and the needy, and understand the words of James, the half-brother of Jesus:

> Pure and undefiled religion before God and the Father is this: to visit orphans and widows in their trouble, and to keep oneself unspotted from the world (James 1:27 NKJV).

These mature believers refuse to serve the spirit of Mammon, but God also is able to bless and prosper their lives and put significant resources in their hands for the purposes of His Kingdom. Maturity is the GOAL OF GOD for every Christian believer. It is the place of fruitfulness, of multiplication and of reward for a person who hungered after God and made serious decisions to make right choices, build right relationships, and to do things right in their lives. I pray this book will provide somewhat of a roadmap to many on this journey to maturity, helping to correct, complement, and complete the way. "May each of us be presented to Christ as a chaste virgin spiritually" (2 Corinthians 11:2 NKJV) and "may our faith be found to His praise, honor and glory at His appearing" (1 Peter 1:7 NKJV) — in Jesus Name. Amen.

ABOUT THE AUTHOR

Dr. Berin Gilfillan is an American minister, businessman, and author. He is the founder and CEO of Good Shepherd Ministries, International. He is widely known as the creator of the International School of Ministry (ISOM). ISOM has been used in over 20,000 training schools in 150 countries and in 85 languages. It is the world's largest video Bible school and has been a proven leadership training curriculum for more than 20 years.

Although he was an American citizen from birth through his mother, he nonetheless grew up in South Africa. After graduating from Hilton College in Kwazulu, Natal, in 1979, he moved to the US. He received a Bachelor of Arts in Communications from the University of Michigan in 1983. He then moved to Virginia Beach, Virginia, where he began working on his Master's degree in Communication from Regent University. After receiving his degree in 1985, Berin married his wife Lisa, and the couple moved to Frankfurt, Germany, to work with evangelist Reinhard Bonnke.

From 1986–1989, Berin worked as the Television Producer at Christ for all Nations (CfaN), where he produced 11 documentaries about the ministry work of Reinhard Bonnke, including *A Blood-Washed Africa* and *Something to Shout About*. He also produced a series on prayer for Reinhard's intercessor, Suzette Hattingh, called *How to Make Intercession a Lifestyle*. He oversaw the huge technical side of Reinhard's massive EuroFire Conferences in the 1980s. He was involved in the sales and distribution of his materials as well. All that work was done out of Frankfurt, Germany, with numerous trips to other parts of Europe, Asia, and throughout Africa.

After his time with Reinhard Bonnke, Berin once again returned to the US, where he went to Fuller Theological Seminary from 1990–1991, studying under Dr. C. Peter Wagner. During this time, Berin created Good Shepherd Ministries, International (GSMI). Under that banner, the Gilfillan family took off for two years of missionary work in Nigeria. There they started 140 video Bible schools with over 4,000 students, and they also pioneered a preschool that is still existent to this day. What they experienced in Nigeria inspired them to create an international video Bible curriculum that could go into any language in the world. Armed with this vision, Berin, Lisa, and their two children, Christina and Jessica, headed back to the USA.

From 1994–2000, GSMI filmed its primary video material, known as the ISOM Core, with over 160 hours of content from teachers such as Joyce Meyer, T.L. Osborn, John Bevere, Jack Hayford, Marilyn Hickey, Reinhard Bonnke, and many more. These productions were filmed before a live church audience at Cottonwood Church in Los Alamitos, California, pastored by Bayless Conley.

From 1997–1999, Berin served as the Children's Pastor at Cottonwood Church. There he oversaw the spiritual needs of more than 1,200 children from the ages of 0 to 12. He also organized curriculum, teacher training, camps, VBS programs, and weekly spiritual development. He managed a large volunteer staff and some paid staff as well.

In 2005 Berin partnered with Chad Daniel (who worked as Television Producer for Joyce Meyer Ministries) to co-create *YouthBytes*, a Curriculum for Teens. Berin and his wife Lisa also run two Montessori preschools.

In 2006, Berin was awarded a Doctor of Ministry from Vision International University in Ramona, California. His doctoral thesis was his book *Unlocking the Abraham Promise*, which deals with multiplication growth in the Global Church.

Berin currently runs GSMI, which has a staff of over 20 people. The office is the hub that feeds content to hundreds of thousands of students around the world. A significant part of his team focus on the development of individual online studies at the website ministrydegree.org but ISOM's most preferred model is church-based Bible schools.

ABOUT THE AUTHOR

GSMI continues to produce many different types of video training productions for Pastors and churches, including a Women's curriculum (WOW), a Business curriculum (Marketplace Module), and a Community Development program (CDBoks). Berin does graduations worldwide, in addition to continuing to develop new content for the global Church. He often leads missions trips and especially tries yearly to take a large group of Christian believers to Israel.

Berin now resides in Redlands, California, with his wife, Lisa. When he's not at work, he enjoys spending time with his granddaughter Liliana.

You can follow him on twitter @ceoisomorg, Facebook @BerinLisaGilfillan, or Instagram @berinsworld.

PURSUING MATURITY

MORE FROM DR. BERIN GILFILLAN

Unlocking the Abraham Promise PAPERBACK
by Dr. Berin Gilfillan

There is a promise in the Scriptures that is available to all Christians, male and female, of all races and economic backgrounds. The promise will bring about massive fruitfulness and blessings in the lives of believers. It guarantees triumphant living overall one's enemies and opens up nation-reaching and nation-blessing potential. The highest oath in the universe backs it, and it is waiting to be unlocked.

"Reading these pages, you will gain a deeper understanding of who you are and the importance of your place in the world, as God's powerful promise and hundredfold blessing to you are unlocked!"

— Dr. Marilyn Hickey

Conquering the Sin Nature AUDIO CD
by Dr. Berin Gilfillan

This lesson on how to overcome the thoughts of your mind took me 13 agonizing years to learn. When I finally got free, I found that what I had learned would also help so many others to have victory in their thought lives. That is why I recorded this teaching.

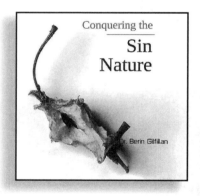

"This message has set many people I know free or on the road to freedom. I gave a copy to my hairdresser. Her son was so changed by it he made copies for many of his friends at High School and used the teaching in the Christian Club. He has now graduated from University and is on fire for God, much due to this teaching."

— Client Testimonial

PURCHASE THESE AND MANY MORE:
shepherdslife.bandcamp.com/merch